AF782527

CONTENTS

ENHANCING BORDER SECURITY AND LAW ENFORCEMENT

HEARING

BEFORE THE

SUBCOMMITTEE ON CRIMINAL JUSTICE, DRUG POLICY AND HUMAN RESOURCES

OF THE

COMMITTEE ON GOVERNMENT REFORM

HOUSE OF REPRESENTATIVES

ONE HUNDRED SEVENTH CONGRESS

SECOND SESSION

APRIL 10, 2002

Serial No. 107–171

Printed for the use of the Committee on Government Reform

Available via the World Wide Web: http://www.gpo.gov/congress/house
http://www.house.gov/reform

U.S. GOVERNMENT PRINTING OFFICE

85–608 PDF WASHINGTON : 2003

For sale by the Superintendent of Documents, U.S. Government Printing Office
Internet: bookstore.gpo.gov Phone: toll free (866) 512–1800; DC area (202) 512–1800
Fax: (202) 512–2250 Mail: Stop SSOP, Washington, DC 20402–0001

COMMITTEE ON GOVERNMENT REFORM

DAN BURTON, Indiana, *Chairman*

BENJAMIN A. GILMAN, New York
CONSTANCE A. MORELLA, Maryland
CHRISTOPHER SHAYS, Connecticut
ILEANA ROS-LEHTINEN, Florida
JOHN M. MCHUGH, New York
STEPHEN HORN, California
JOHN L. MICA, Florida
THOMAS M. DAVIS, Virginia
MARK E. SOUDER, Indiana
STEVEN C. LATOURETTE, Ohio
BOB BARR, Georgia
DAN MILLER, Florida
DOUG OSE, California
RON LEWIS, Kentucky
JO ANN DAVIS, Virginia
TODD RUSSELL PLATTS, Pennsylvania
DAVE WELDON, Florida
CHRIS CANNON, Utah
ADAM H. PUTNAM, Florida
C.L. "BUTCH" OTTER, Idaho
EDWARD L. SCHROCK, Virginia
JOHN J. DUNCAN, JR., Tennessee
——— ———

HENRY A. WAXMAN, California
TOM LANTOS, California
MAJOR R. OWENS, New York
EDOLPHUS TOWNS, New York
PAUL E. KANJORSKI, Pennsylvania
PATSY T. MINK, Hawaii
CAROLYN B. MALONEY, New York
ELEANOR HOLMES NORTON, Washington, DC
ELIJAH E. CUMMINGS, Maryland
DENNIS J. KUCINICH, Ohio
ROD R. BLAGOJEVICH, Illinois
DANNY K. DAVIS, Illinois
JOHN F. TIERNEY, Massachusetts
JIM TURNER, Texas
THOMAS H. ALLEN, Maine
JANICE D. SCHAKOWSKY, Illinois
WM. LACY CLAY, Missouri
DIANE E. WATSON, California
STEPHEN F. LYNCH, Massachusetts
———
BERNARD SANDERS, Vermont (Independent)

KEVIN BINGER, *Staff Director*
DANIEL R. MOLL, *Deputy Staff Director*
JAMES C. WILSON, *Chief Counsel*
ROBERT A. BRIGGS, *Chief Clerk*
PHIL SCHILIRO, *Minority Staff Director*

SUBCOMMITTEE ON CRIMINAL JUSTICE, DRUG POLICY AND HUMAN RESOURCES

MARK E. SOUDER, Indiana, *Chairman*

BENJAMIN A. GILMAN, New York
ILEANA ROS-LEHTINEN, Florida
JOHN L. MICA, Florida,
BOB BARR, Georgia
DAN MILLER, Florida
DOUG OSE, California
JO ANN DAVIS, Virginia
DAVE WELDON, Florida

ELIJAH E. CUMMINGS, Maryland
ROD R. BLAGOJEVICH, Illinois
BERNARD SANDERS, Vermont
DANNY K. DAVIS, Illinois
JIM TURNER, Texas
THOMAS H. ALLEN, Maine
JANICE D. SCHAKOWKY, Illinois

EX OFFICIO

DAN BURTON, Indiana
HENRY A. WAXMAN, California

CHRISTOPHER DONESA, *Staff Director*
NICHOLAS COLEMAN, *Counsel*
CONN CARROLL, *Clerk*
JULIAN A. HAYWOOD, *Minority Counsel*

ENHANCING BORDER SECURITY AND LAW ENFORCEMENT

WEDNESDAY, APRIL 10, 2002

HOUSE OF REPRESENTATIVES,
SUBCOMMITTEE ON CRIMINAL JUSTICE, DRUG POLICY AND HUMAN RESOURCES,
COMMITTEE ON GOVERNMENT REFORM,
Washington, DC.

The subcommittee met, pursuant to notice, at 10:05 a.m., in room 2514, Rayburn House Office Building, Hon. Mark E. Souder (chairman of the subcommittee) presiding.

Present: Representatives Souder, Cummings and Davis.

Staff present: Nicholas Coleman, counsel; Christopher Donessa, staff director and chief counsel; Conn Carroll, clerk; Tony Haywood, minority counsel; and Earley Green, minority assistant clerk.

Mr. SOUDER. The subcommittee will now come to order. Good morning. Thank you all for coming. Today our subcommittee will investigate various proposals to enhance border security and law enforcement.

Since last summer this subcommittee has been conducting a comprehensive study of our Nation's borders, considering ways to improve both security and the efficient flow of international commerce, travel and tourism.

As policymakers have looked at ways to improve security at the border, a variety of significant, even sweeping changes have been suggested. These new proposals have involved both new technologies and new strategies to be used in inspections, in new organizational structures for agencies involved in border law enforcement.

Four of these proposals merit special attention here today. First, the ramifications of moving our emphasis away from cargo inspections at the border toward inspections at the point of origin. In theory this would speed cargo through the ports of entry and eliminate what could be substantial delays as well as allow Customs inspectors to focus their inspection efforts on high risk cargo shipments.

As the sheer volume of cargo shipments increases, it is clear that dramatically increasing preclearances will be required. Several issues need to be resolved, however. First, since these inspections must take place on foreign soil, how much control over the process can U.S. Customs officials actually exercise?

Second, how will precleared cargo be protected from tampering as it is transported to the United States? In addition, how will the extra cost of inspecting, protecting and monitoring precleared cargo be allocated? Will the Federal Government pick up the tab or will the industry be forced to bear the cost and pass it on to American consumers?

These and other questions must be answered before undertaking such a fundamental shift in law enforcement strategy.

Second, we will examine the related issue of expediting the movement of travelers. The Customs Service and the INS have already set up so-called Fast Pass systems for commuters on both the Northern and Southern borders. On the Northern border, the NEXUS system is a joint project between the United States and Canada, under which frequent commuters can enroll in a program that allows them to use dedicated lanes, skip the long lines faced by other border crossers.

On the Southern border, the SENTRI system allows both the American and Mexican citizens to use a dedicated commuter lane after submitting to a background check and paying a user fee.

At each of our field hearings, residents of border communities have pressed for the expansion of these programs.

Again, several issues need to be addressed before the decision to expand significant resources on the Fastpass systems is made. Canada and Mexico do not have equally efficient mechanisms for background checks. Also, it is not yet clear that fastpass lanes have had a significant beneficial impact on the amount of traffic in the general inspection lanes. Before removing further lanes from use by the general public, we should be certain that the Fastpass system will help the overall traffic situation.

Finally, while the SENTRI system is at least partially funded by user fees on the Southern border, currently no user fee is collected on the Northern border. One significant question, therefore, is whether the fastpass systems should be paid for by all of the taxpayers or by those who use the systems.

Third. Both Customs and the INS are moving forward with the modernization of their computer data bases and automated systems. Customs faces the daunting challenge of replacing the Automated Commercial System [ACS], which was first developed in 1984, with the Automated Commercial Environment [ACE].

ACS was designed to keep track of commercial shipments into the United States and to help Customs target which shipments should be inspected for contraband. The system is antiquated, however, and it frequently crashes. Planning for ACE began in 1990, but as yet no system has been finalized. It appears it will take at least another 5 years before it is up and running.

While there is broad agreement that ACS is inadequate and that ACE must be deployed as soon as is feasible, Congress needs to know now how much the new system will cost and how quickly and widely it can be deployed.

Finally, several proposals have been made to consolidate the various agencies responsible for border management. The most sweeping proposals have been made in the Senate where one bill envisions merging Customs, INS, the Department of Transportation and other agencies into a Department of Homeland Security.

A less ambitious proposal reportedly under consideration by the administration would merge Customs, the Border Patrol and INS's enforcement divisions into a single agency under the supervision of the Department of Justice.

While consolidation of border enforcement agencies should be given appropriate consideration, much more information will be needed before such a step can be confidently taken. Consolidating even just the INS and Customs would require significant time and effort and would only be justified if both agencies would benefit.

Congress needs specific information about what problems would be solved by the agency merger, what activities would be enhanced, and what difficulties caused by the merger would have to be overcome. These issues are all extremely important. And I look forward to discussing them with all of our witnesses today.

[The prepared statement of Hon. Mark E. Souder follows:]

Opening Statement
Chairman Mark Souder

"Enhancing Border Security and Law Enforcement"

Subcommittee on Criminal Justice, Drug Policy, and Human Resources
Committee on Government Reform

April 10, 2002

Good morning and thank you all for coming. Today our Subcommittee will investigate various proposals to enhance border security and law enforcement. Since last summer, this Subcommittee has been conducting a comprehensive study of our nation's borders, considering ways to improve both security and the efficient flow of international commerce, travel and tourism. We have focused particular attention on the U.S. Customs Service, the Immigration and Naturalization Service and the U.S. Border Patrol, which are the agencies chiefly responsible for protecting our borders and ports of entry against the continuing threats of drug smuggling, illegal immigration and terrorism.

As policymakers have looked at ways to improve security at the border, a variety of significant, even sweeping changes have been suggested. These new proposals have involved both new technologies and new strategies to be used in inspections, and new organizational structures for the agencies involved in border law enforcement. Four of these proposals merit special attention here today.

First, one of the most important changes being contemplated is a shift away from cargo inspections at the border towards inspections at the "point of origin." The Customs Service has launched several new pilot programs to pre-clear cargo at the place where it is packaged and shipped, allowing it to pass through our borders without additional inspections. In theory, this system would solve two related problems: first, it would speed cargo through the ports of entry, thus eliminating what can be substantial delays;

second, and more importantly, it would allow Customs inspectors to focus their inspection efforts on high-risk cargo shipments.

As the sheer volume of cargo shipments increases it is clear that some form of pre-clearance will be required. Several issues need to be resolved, however. First, since point of origin inspections must take place on foreign soil, how much control over the process can U.S. Customs officials actually exercise? Second, how will pre-cleared cargo be protected from tampering as it is transported to the U.S.? In addition, how will the costs of inspecting, protecting and monitoring pre-cleared cargo be allocated – will the federal government pick up the tab, or will the industry be forced to bear the cost, and pass it on to American consumers? These and other questions must be answered before undertaking such a fundamental shift in law enforcement strategy.

Second, we will examine the related issue of pre-clearance of travelers. The Customs Service and the INS have already set up so-called "fastpass" systems for commuters on both the Northern and Southern borders. On the Northern border, the NEXUS system is a joint project between the U.S. and Canada, under which frequent commuters can enroll in a program that allows them to use a dedicated lane and skip the long lines faced by other border crossers. On the Southern border, the SENTRI system allows both American and Mexican citizens to use a dedicated commuter lane after submitting to a background check and paying a user fee. At each of our field hearings, residents of border communities have pressed for the expansion of these programs.

Again, several issues need to be addressed before the decision to expend significant resources on fastpass systems is made. First, while criminal background checks of Canadian citizens can easily be made using Canada's centralized databases, the same is not true for Mexican citizens, since Mexico lacks a unified criminal database. Instead, the INS and Customs have been forced to rely on letters from local police chiefs in Mexico, certifying that a particular individual does not have a criminal history. If fastpass systems are expanded on the Southern border, this problem needs to be addressed, because the more people are enrolled, the greater the risk that drug smugglers or other criminals will attempt to take advantage of it. Second, it is not yet clear that fastpass lanes have had a significant beneficial impact on the amount of traffic in the general inspection lanes. Before removing further lanes from use by the general public, we should be certain that the fastpass system will help the overall traffic situation. Finally, while the SENTRI system is at least partially funded by user fees on the Southern border, currently no user fee is collected on the Northern border. One significant question therefore is whether fastpass systems should be paid for by taxpayers, or by those who use the systems.

Third, both Customs and the INS are moving forward with the modernization of their computer databases and automated systems. Customs in particular faces the daunting challenge of replacing the Automated Commercial System (ACS), which was first developed in 1984, with the Automated Commercial Environment (ACE). ACS was designed to keep track of commercial shipments into the U.S., and to help Customs target which shipments should be inspected for contraband. The system is antiquated, however, and it frequently crashes. Planning for ACE began in 1990, but as yet no system has been finalized, and it appears it will take at least another 5 years before it is up and running. While there is broad agreement that ACS is inadequate and that ACE must be deployed as soon as is feasible, Congress needs to know how much the new system will cost, and how quickly and widely it can be deployed.

Finally, several proposals have been made to consolidate the various agencies responsible for border management. The most sweeping proposals have been made in the Senate, where one bill envisions merging Customs, INS, the Department of Transportation, and other agencies into a Department of Homeland Security. A less ambitious proposal, reportedly under consideration by the Administration, would merge Customs, the Border Patrol, and INS' enforcement divisions into a single agency under the supervision of the Department of Justice. While consolidation of border enforcement agencies should be given appropriate consideration, much more information will be needed before such a step can be confidently taken. Consolidating even just the INS and Customs would require significant time and effort, and would only be justified if both agencies would benefit. Congress needs specific information about what problems would be solved by agency merger, what activities would be enhanced, and what difficulties caused by the merger would have to be overcome.

These issues are all extremely important, and I look forward to discussing them with all of our witnesses today. We are pleased to welcome Ms. Bonni Tischler, Assistant Commissioner of the Office of Field Operations, U.S. Customs Service; Mr. Larry C. Johnson, CEO and Founder of BERG Associates LLC, and a former counter-terrorism expert at the CIA and the Department of State; Ms. Colleen M. Kelley, National President of the National Treasury Employees Union, which represents Customs workers; Mr. T.J. Bonner, President of the National Border Patrol Council of the American Federation of Government Employees, which represents INS employees; Mr. Christopher Koch **[pronounced COOK]**, President of the World Shipping Council; Mr. John Simpson, President of the American Association of Exporters and Importers; and Mr. Steve Russell, Chairman and CEO of Celadon Trucking Services, representing the American Trucking Associations. We thank everyone for taking the time this morning to join us for this important discussion.

Mr. SOUDER. We are pleased to welcome Ms. Bonni Tischler, Assistant Commissioner of the Office of Field Operations for the U.S. Customs Service; Mr. Larry Johnson, CEO and Founder of BERG Associates, LLC, and a former counterterrorism expert at the CIA and the Department of State; Ms. Colleen Kelley, National President of the National Treasury Employees Union, which represents Customs workers; Mr. T. J. Bonner, President of the National Border Patrol Council of the American Federation of Government Employees which represents the INS employees; Mr. Christopher Koch, President of the World Shipping Council; Mr. John Simpson, President of the American Association of Exporters and Importers; and Mr. Steve Russell, Chairman and CEO of Celadon Trucking Services, representing the American Trucking Associations.

We thank everyone for taking the time this morning to join us for this important discussion.

Now I would like to recognize Mr. Cummings for an opening statement.

Mr. CUMMINGS. Thank you very much, Mr. Chairman. I want to commend you for holding this hearing and for taking such a keen interest in the issue of promoting security and efficiency at America's border crossings and ports of entry.

The series of field hearings you have held, culminating in today's hearing, serve an important purpose. Our air, land, and seaports of entry are literally America's gateways to travel, tourism and international trade and commerce.

Our desire for openness and cultural exchange and our dependence on international trade, make it imperative that these conduits operate efficiently.

But as the persistent illegal narcotics trade and, even more dramatically, the September 11th attacks have demonstrated, our insistence upon openness can be manipulated to inflict tragic consequences upon us all. Because of the nature of the September 11th attacks, the issue of airport security and airplane passenger safety has drawn enormous attention from the public, the media and all levels of government, and rightly so.

Equally important, however, is our government's responsibility to ensure that America's land and seaports are able to operate both safely and efficiently. That is the reason for today's hearing. The more than 40 Federal agencies that operate at our Nation's ports of entry have an enormous task on their collective hands. Among those, the burden of regulating our borders and ports and providing the first line of defense in our homeland security efforts.

This falls heaviest upon the U.S. Customs Service, the Immigration and Naturalization Service, the U.S. Coast Guard and the U.S. Border Patrol. We will hear directly today only from the Customs Service, but all of our witnesses will have something to say about the efforts of all of these agencies and how they can work most effectively and efficiently together to advance the Nation's interest in securing our borders, facilitating tourism and trade, and enforcing our laws.

Mr. Chairman, I must say that I do regret that we don't have the director of the Office of Homeland Security, Tom Ridge, who is the person who brings all of this together and could probably provide us with the kind of information we need, here today with us.

As you all are aware, Mr. Chairman, Customs Service Chairman Bonner recently said that if terrorists succeeded in detonating a nuclear device in a commercial shipping container, the government would shut our container terminals down.

Leaving aside the tragic health and environmental consequences of such an event, I suspect that many Americans do not realize the extent to which the American economy is supported by its seaports. The Port of Baltimore, for example, contributes mightily to the economic strength of the Mid Atlantic region in particular. But the goods that arrive there reach deep into the Midwest and other areas of the country, just as the goods that leave through it travel all over the world. Cities like Baltimore, New Orleans, New York and Los Angeles that have major commercial ports depend on those ports to support a wide array of related industries that employ millions of Americans both locally and far beyond their borders.

The shutting down of just one major U.S. port would have a substantial national economic impact and ripples would be felt worldwide. Similarly, the flow of commerce over land between the United States and our two largest trading partners, Mexico and Canada, is vital to the economic health of the entire hemisphere and beyond.

In the new normality that has been thrust upon us, Customs, INS, Border Patrol and the Coast Guard are all being forced to evolve quickly to meet the challenge of avoiding the kind of threat to homeland security and the world economy that Commissioner Bonner described.

New initiatives in the area of technology, strategy and interagency cooperation, including a possible reorganization of so-called border agencies, are being developed, implemented or considered by Congress and the administration.

Today's hearing provides an important opportunity to examine both the status and the wisdom of these various efforts, and I look forward to hearing the valuable testimony of our witnesses.

With that, Mr. Chairman, I yield back and I thank you.

Mr. SOUDER. Thank you. Before proceeding, I would first like to have the record show that the director of Homeland Security, Mr. Ridge, will be giving a briefing to the members of this full committee this week, and we are looking forward to that. Mr. Zigler has been in front of us several times. They have a number of hearings on the Hill, will continue to work with INS.

Today we will be focusing a little more directly on the commerce interaction which is more directly related to Customs, but we will have a number of INS questions, and they have submitted written testimony and will respond to our questions as those directly showing to overlap as well.

Mr. CUMMINGS. Will the chairman yield for a question?

Mr. SOUDER. I yield for a question.

Mr. CUMMINGS. Just one question. On Tom Ridge's appearance before that committee, that is—before our committee, is that closed? Is that the entire committee? Is that a closed hearing? Will the public have access?

Mr. SOUDER. Yes. My understanding is that it is—double-check because I assumed it was closed, which it is. But it is for the full committee.

Mr. CUMMINGS. Very well. Thank you.

Mr. SOUDER. But that—we formally invited, but did not pressure Mr. Ridge to come in public because we knew the briefing was coming. But he is clearly going to need to speak to the Hill more in response if in fact consolidation goes ahead. I think both sides agree with that basic point.

Before proceeding, I would like to take care of a couple of procedural matters. First, I would ask unanimous consent that all Members have 5 legislative days to submit written statements and questions for the hearing record and that any answers to written questions provided by the witnesses also be included in the record.

Without objection, it is so ordered.

Second, I ask unanimous consent that all exhibits, documents and other materials referred to by the Members and the witnesses may be included in the hearing record, and that all Members be permitted to revise and extend their remarks. Without objection, it is so ordered.

As is customary, we will begin with the administration witness who today is Ms. Bonni Tischler, Assistant Commissioner for the Office of Field Operations for the U.S. Customs Service.

I would like to note for the record that we also invited the representatives of INS and the White House, as I just said. There are a number of other hearings. We know there are pressures on all of the witnesses and we appreciate it very much that the Customs has come today, because we have this focus on commerce. It is a standard in our committee to ask all witnesses to testify under oath. So, Ms. Tischler, if you would stand and raise your right hand.

[Witness sworn.]

Mr. SOUDER. Let the record show that the witness responded in the affirmative. I now ask you to give an opening statement. We ask you to summarize it in 5 minutes. We will insert your full statement in the record.

STATEMENT OF BONNI TISCHLER, ASSISTANT COMMISSIONER, OFFICE OF FIELD OPERATIONS, U.S. CUSTOMS SERVICE

Ms. TISCHLER. Thank you, Mr. Chairman and members of the subcommittee, for this opportunity to testify on behalf of Commissioner Bonner and the U.S. Customs Service. Throughout our 212-year history, the Customs Service has demonstrated its ability to adapt to the varying challenges our Nation has faced in its greatest times of peril.

With the tragic events of September 11th, a coordinated attack on our homeland, the mission of the Customs Service has evolved yet again. And simply put, our No. 1 priority is now to protect our Nation from terrorists.

The task at hand is enormous. On a national basis the Customs Service is responsible for processing over 470 million people, 129 million cars and over 19 million trucks, railcars and sea containers that arrive into the United States each year. Obviously we cannot inspect each and every shipment of goods that enters the United States. To do so would cripple the flow of trade.

Customs employs a systematic process based on the principles of risk management. This process involves data collection and analysis, combined with years of experience and old fashioned intuition as our personnel identify trends and anomalies in data to make informed risk-based decisions on what to screen, target and, when appropriate, examine.

Since September 11th the Customs Service has been operating at our highest level of vigilance. Inspectors manning America's front line have been staffing land border ports of entry around the clock, performing increased enforcement screenings, examinations and security operations.

Officers at our ports of entry are working 12 to 16 hours a day, 6 and 7 days a week, and they have been doing so for over 6 months. Since last September the rules have changed. Customs can no longer be satisfied with conducting examinations solely at the port of entry. We must begin to view the border as more than a mere physical boundary between countries. We must also understand it in terms of the actions we undertake with our foreign partners to prescreen people and goods before they arrive in the United States.

To better address the threat that terrorists could exploit commercial trade, Customs has developed a Container Security Initiative. We call it CSI, which is designed to improve our border security and efficiency by pushing our enforcement efforts beyond our borders.

CSI will allow U.S. Customs more time to anticipate, identify and stop threats before they reach our shores and expedite the flow of low risk commerce across our borders. The core elements of this initiative include receiving specific advance electronic manifest information, establishing a common targeting methodology for identifying high risk containers, and prescreening these containers at their port of departure before they are loaded aboard a vessel and transported to the United States.

CSI is already underway. Customs has personnel detailed to seaports in Montreal, Halifax and Vancouver, Canada to target intransit sea containers destined to the United States. In order for our efforts to push our border outward under CSI to be successful, we must enlist the support of industry and the trade community.

To this end, Customs announced the development of the Customs Trade Partnership Against Terrorism, CTPAT, and Operation Shield America. Through CTPAT we are working with importers, carriers and other industry sectors to secure the international supply chain by emphasizing a seamless security-conscious environment throughout the entire commercial process. Operation Shield America is an industry outreach initiative dedicated to enlisting the support of manufacturers and distributors in preventing terrorist organizations from obtaining weapons or sensitive equipment and technologies.

Furthermore, Customs is leading Operation Green Quest, a multiagency initiative aimed at interdicting terrorist funding by identifying, disrupting and dismantling the financial systems they use to fund their operations.

Through interagency efforts, working with our law enforcement counterparts and members of industry, we are developing comprehensive strategies, procedures and plans to maximize the utilization of existing resources to improve border security, coordinate enforcement activity and respond to terrorist acts and collaborate on legislative initiatives.

On the international front, Customs is working with our counterparts in Canada and Mexico to improve the level and information exchange and adopt measures to protect our mutual borders.

Over 25 initiatives aimed at improving cross-border collaboration and security are already underway under the Smart Border Accord recently signed with Canada. A similar agreement was recently negotiated with Mexico and we are in the initial stages of developing eight joint action plans to address security issues along the southwest border.

Customs' most important technology initiative to secure our future was already underway before the events of September 11th. This initiative is the ongoing development of the automated commercial environment or ACE. ACE will provide the information technology architecture and infrastructure that will allow Customs to streamline our commercial data processing systems and significantly improve our ability to collect advance commercial information from a variety of automated sources in order to efficiently perform law enforcement analysis and targeting.

Technology and information-sharing are absolutely essential to our counterterrorist mission. Customs must deploy the technology necessary to rapidly and comprehensively inspect arriving and departing conveyances and cargo at our ports of entry in order to detect anomalies and prevent the smuggling of weapons of mass destruction, narcotics and other contraband. This must be done without impeding the flow of legitimate commercial trade. Customs is implementing a strategy to develop, acquire and deploy non-intrusive INS technology to systematically increase the smuggler's risk of detection in all port environments, including all modes of transportation.

So far under this plan Customs has deployed over 80 large scale inspection systems at our air, land and seaports of entry. These large-scale fixed sites, relocateable and mobile X-ray and gamma ray imaging systems are able to rapidly and efficiently screen commercial trucks, sea containers and vehicles entering the United States.

In addition to these large-scale systems, Customs has also deployed personal radiation detectors to allow inspectors to monitor their ports for radioactive sources. We are also working on developing new smart technologies capable of ensuring the integrity of a shipment and those capable of detecting and identifying chemical, biological and nuclear materials. For example, U.S. Customs and the Department of Transportation are in the initial stages of trying to develop a secure technology, a smart seal, capable of ensuring the integrity of a sea container or alerting law enforcement personnel when tampering has occurred.

Additionally, we are also working on the development of wireless technology like personal data assistants and notebook computers which can interface with our law enforcement data bases on the ground. This wireless technology will improve the flow and exchange of key law enforcement data to ensure our officers on the front line have the most current tactical information available to them when they are performing enforcement operations to target and examine high risk passengers and cargo shipments.

In closing, allow me to state that we are grateful for this support we have received from the administration and Congress to continue the development of ACE. We also appreciate the support we recently received in the antiterrorism supplemental budget which will provide additional inspectors, agents and K–9 enforcement officers and more high-tech, nonintrusive INS technology for deployment at our ports of entry over the next 2 years.

I firmly believe that the U.S. Customs Service has the expertise and the experience to protect our borders. Thank you again, Mr. Chairman, and the members of the subcommittee for this opportunity to testify. I look forward to answering any questions you may have.

[The prepared statement of Ms. Tischler follows:]

**TESTIMONY OF BONNI G. TISCHLER
ASSISTANT COMMISSIONER
OFFICE OF FIELD OPERATIONS
UNITED STATES CUSTOMS SERVICE
BEFORE
THE COMMITTEE ON GOVERNMENT REFORM
SUBCOMMITTEE ON CRIMINAL JUSTICE, DRUG POLICY, AND
HUMAN RESOURCES**

Thank you Mr. Chairman and members of the Subcommittee for this opportunity to testify on behalf of Commissioner Bonner and the United States Customs Service.

Throughout our 212-year history, the Customs Service has demonstrated its ability to adapt to the varying challenges our nation has faced in its greatest times of peril. With the tragic events of September 11th, a coordinated attack on our homeland, the mission of the Customs Service has evolved yet again - - simply put, our number one priority is now to protect our nation from terrorists.

The task at hand is enormous. On a national basis, the Customs Service is responsible for processing over 470 million people, 129 million cars, and over 19 million trucks, railcars and sea containers that arrive into the United States each year.

Obviously, we cannot inspect each and every shipment of goods that enters the United States. To do so would cripple the flow of trade. Customs employs a systematic process based on the principles of risk management. This process involves data collection and analysis combined with years of experience and old-fashioned intuition, as our personnel identify trends and anomalies in data to make informed, risk-based decisions on what to screen, target, and, when appropriate, - - examine.

Since September 11th, the Customs Service has been operating at Alert Level 1, our highest level of vigilance. Inspectors manning America's frontline have been staffing land border ports of entry 24 hours a day, performing increased enforcement screenings, examinations and security operations. Individual officers at our ports of entry are working 12 to 16 hour shifts, six to seven days a week, and they have been doing so for over six months. In fact, our drug seizures are up considerably as a result of our heightened state of alert.

Organizational Steps to Improve Security and Efficiency

Since last September, the rules have changed. Customs can no longer be satisfied with conducting examinations solely at the port of entry. We must begin to view "the border" as more than a mere physical boundary between countries. We must also understand it in terms of the actions we undertake with our foreign partners to prescreen people and goods before they arrive in the United States.

To better address the threat, that terrorists could exploit commercial trade, Customs has developed a Container Security Initiative (CSI) which is designed to improve our border security and efficiency by pushing our enforcement efforts beyond our borders. CSI will allow U.S. Customs more time to anticipate, identify and stop threats before they reach our shores -- and expedite the flow of low-risk commerce across our borders.

The core elements of this initiative include receiving specific advance electronic manifest information, establishing a common targeting methodology for identifying high-risk containers, and pre-screening these containers at their departure ports, **before** they are loaded aboard a vessel and transported to the United States.

CSI is already underway. Customs has personnel detailed to seaports in Montreal, Halifax and Vancouver, Canada, to target in-transit sea containers destined to the United States. Canadian officers are on detail to two U.S. seaports (Seattle, Washington and Newark, New Jersey) performing similar targeting functions.

In order for our efforts to push our border outward under CSI to be successful, we must enlist the support of the industry and trade community. To this end, Customs announced the development of the Customs - Trade Partnership Against Terrorism (C-TPAT) and Operation Shield America. Through C-TPAT, we are working with importers, carriers and other industry sectors to secure the international supply chain by emphasizing a seamless security conscious environment throughout the entire commercial process. Operation Shield America is an industry outreach initiative dedicated to enlisting the support of manufacturers and distributors in preventing terrorist organizations from obtaining weapons or sensitive equipment and technologies.

However, Customs cannot act alone to address the terrorist threat our nation faces. We have been working in conjunction with other key border security stakeholders like the Office of Homeland Security, the Immigration and Naturalization Service, and the U.S. Coast Guard as well as our international partners in Canada and Mexico.

On the homefront, Customs is actively engaged in a joint U.S. Customs - Department of Transportation Container Working Group aimed at improving the security of sea containers entering our nation. Just last week, this working group presented a report containing short and long-term recommendations to improve sea container security to the Office of Homeland Security. Additionally, we are also participating in a multi-agency effort to develop a joint border security plan. We are in the process of finalizing this joint border security plan right now.

Furthermore, Customs is leading Operation Green Quest, a multi-agency initiative aimed at interdicting terrorist funding by identifying, disrupting and dismantling the financial systems they use to fund their operations.

Through these inter-agency efforts, working with our law enforcement counterparts, and members of industry we are developing comprehensive strategies, procedures and plans to maximize the utilization of existing resources and improve border security; coordinate enforcement activity and responses to terrorist acts; and collaborate on legislative initiatives.

On the International front, Customs is working with our counterparts in Canada and Mexico to improve the level of information exchange and adopt measures to protect our mutual borders. Over 25 initiatives aimed at improving cross border collaboration and security are already underway under the Smart Border Accord recently signed with Canada. A similar agreement was recently negotiated with Mexico and we are in the initial stages of developing 8 joint action plans to address security issues along the Southwest border.

Development of Technology to Secure Our Future

Customs' most important technology initiative to secure our future was already underway before the events of September 11th. This initiative is the ongoing development of the Automated Commercial Environment (ACE). ACE replaces the aging Automated Commercial System (ACS), and will provide the information technology architecture and infrastructure that will allow Customs to streamline our commercial data processing systems. ACE will allow Customs greater efficiencies and economies of scale and significantly improve our ability to collect advance commercial information from a variety of automated sources in order to perform law enforcement analysis and targeting.

International Trade Data System (ITDS) as an integrated part of ACE, is intended to streamline Government and provide a single interface for trading partners who must submit import and export data to the U.S. Government. ITDS will provide benefits to participating government agencies and the trade. The benefits will include single window filing for trade information, improved enforcement of, and compliance with, trade requirements, and an improved multi-agency database for security assessments. Customs will continue to develop ACE and internal ITDS requirements.

ACE is a priority of the Customs Service. It is essential to our overall security plan, and it is critically important that the successful and timely design, funding and implementation of ACE take place. This system was planned to be fully operational in 5 years. Commissioner Bonner believes that we should make every effort to complete ACE in 4 years.

Technology and information sharing are essential to our counter-terrorist mission. Customs must deploy the technology necessary to rapidly and comprehensively inspect arriving and departing conveyances and cargo at our ports of entry to detect anomalies and prevent the smuggling of weapons of mass destruction, narcotics and other contraband. This must be done without impeding the flow of legitimate commercial traffic. To achieve this, Customs has developed a strategy to develop, acquire and deploy non-intrusive inspection technology to systematically increase the smugglers risk of detection in all port environments including all modes of transportation. To date, Customs has deployed 81 large-scale non-intrusive inspection (NII) systems at our air, land and sea ports of entry, and is expanding its NII technology with resources available in the FY '02 supplemental and requested in the FY 03 budget request.

These large scale fixed-site, relocateable and mobile x-ray and gamma-ray imaging systems are able to rapidly and efficiently screen commercial trucks, sea containers and vehicles entering the United States increasing our enforcement capability. In addition to these large scale systems, Customs has also deployed over 3,800 Personal Radiation Detectors (PRDs) to allow inspectors to monitor their area for radioactive sources. We have developed a plan to procure and deploy PRD equipment for each inspector.

However, merely detecting anomalies will not totally address the threat we now face. As a result, we are working on developing new "smart" technologies capable of ensuring the integrity of a shipment; and those capable of detecting and identifying chemical, biological, and nuclear materials. For example, U.S. Customs and the Department of Transportation are in the initial stages of trying to develop a secure technology (a smart seal) capable of ensuring the integrity of a sea container or alerting law enforcement personnel when tampering has occurred.

We are also researching the development of wireless technology like Personal Data Assistants (PDAs) and notebook computers, which can interface with our main law enforcement databases like the Treasury Enforcement Communication System (TECS). This wireless technology will improve the flow and exchange of key law enforcement information to ensure our officers on the front line have the most current data available to them when they are performing enforcement operations to target and examine high-risk passengers and cargo shipments.

Development of this type of technology will promote accountability and shipment integrity as it moves through the international supply chain.

However, in developing this cutting edge technology, it is important that we remain cognizant of the possible cost and logistics implications in order to ensure that the technology solution is cost effective, and promotes the expeditious processing of persons, conveyances and goods across our nation's border. We will remain vigilant in this endeavor to develop technology that is both affordable and effective.

Conclusion

In closing, allow me to state that we are grateful for the support we have received from the Administration and Congress to continue the development of ACE. We also appreciate the support we recently received in the anti-terrorism supplemental budget which will provide additional Inspectors and Canine Enforcement Officers and more hi-tech non-intrusive inspection technology for deployment at our sea and land border ports of entry over the next two years. I firmly believe that the U.S. Customs Service has the expertise and the experience to protect our borders. Working with our law enforcement counterparts, members of the international community and the industry, we are developing and implementing a plan to extend our nation's borders to deter terrorists who would target America.

Thank you again, Mr. Chairman and the members of the Subcommittee, for this opportunity to testify. I look forward to answering any questions you may have.

Mr. SOUDER. Thank you very much for both your leadership and your willingness to testify today. The challenges that the Customs Service is facing are overwhelming. Just the daunting challenges that you faced in commerce and contraband and illegals before was difficult enough and stressing our system even before we got into the September 11th.

So far I have been on both the north and south borders. In Vermont, in addition to looking for Quebec Gold and ecstacy, they are looking for contraband cheese coming across.

In North Dakota, I went through one of the facilities for the train inspections that is relatively new. They have a lot of cargo, wheat, moving across, and other things across the North Dakota border where we have more crossings, actually, than any other place in the United States. In Los Angeles, Long Beach, some of the new technology that Customs has brought in there at the largest harbors in the world, it is amazing the different things you have to look for and what the Customs agents in the field have to look for, and they vary so dramatically, even from site to site, even in the same State range.

We are working on this border report. I have a number of very specific questions. We will probably do two rounds here and then submit some others for written. One of the—maybe I will start with the automated computer system. What is the time table roughly for implementation, and how long before it is deployed at the seaports and the airports as well as the border crossings?

Ms. TISCHLER. Well, our automated commercial environment is actually just that, an environment. So it is not just a rollout to the ports. It is going to encompass everything Customs does commercially. We were on a 5-year timeframe. Our commissioner is doing everything possible to reduce that to 4 years. It is a function of the funding stream. We have been very fortunate the last couple of years, and we look forward to mutually discussing this with your committee and others that in fact are interested in it.

What that commercial environment will do, as I stated before, is really establish an electronic data warehouse. And so while we will be able to efficiently process commercial entries, we will also be able to use it, in conjunction with our targeting system, to identify anomalies in the flow. That is what it is all about. Because whether you are smuggling narcotics or smuggling weapons of mass destruction, it is all about smuggling. And that is the daunting task of how in the sea environment, for instance, to reduce this 5.9 million containers a year to a manageable number for us to in fact effectively look at.

Mr. SOUDER. Do you—when you say 5 to 4, was that starting with fiscal 2001?

Ms. TISCHLER. It is starting fiscal year 2000. But the money was delayed, so I believe they started it in 2001. I know that our first entry configuration is due to start rolling out the end of this year in the beginning of next fiscal year.

Mr. SOUDER. So under that plan it would probably be 2005 if we got accelerated to 4?

Ms. TISCHLER. Yes, sir.

Mr. SOUDER. Do you believe that as we have looked—because we have been at Port Huron as well as San Diego and other places.

But particularly where the SENTRI and the NEXUS systems are, do you believe—and in Blaine, do you believe that they have—do you have figures that show they—that they are succeeding in the way that they had hoped?

Ms. TISCHLER. First, let me state that Commissioner Bonner supports the idea of having these types of fast lanes. You know, we are walking a tightrope. I know I do not have to tell you because you saw it on the Northern and Southern border. Not only facilitating trade, but an enormous number of people cross every day for work and for other reasons, to contribute to the economy, for instance, in Detroit.

Personally I think they should shrink it down to one manageable system. I think at the end of the day our partners in Canada are very pro for that, in fact, that NEXUS and actually the SENTRI environment continue. I think it is part of the Smart Border Accord. So for the people who are crossing now, we think it is pretty efficient. For the numbers that might cross at some point where we would expand the system, it is a question of logistics at that point, is how to create the fast lanes that would allow them to come in.

Port Huron, it is a lot easier, for instance, than at the Port of Detroit.

Mr. SOUDER. That is one of the—I have got some detailed other areas I want to get into in the second round. But we are going to do a little bit of some followup questions, if not today then in writing, on that very problem. Because where have you have—like at Blaine, Washington, you can bounce certain people over to the next port of entry because they are relatively close. On the North Dakota border, New York and Vermont even, but when you get into the matter of the traffic coming through Detroit, it is so jammed that unless we can figure out alternative ways to put it on the Canadian side—Buffalo is the same thing. They have environment challenges about new bridges, and yet Detroit and Buffalo are where the bulk of where the north border traffic is coming through.

On the south border we have a few similar problems, have got a couple of ports of entry where there is longer distances involved. And so we need in Congress to understand, because all of us agree we have to keep the commerce moving and control the terrorism, because jobs and security are our two biggest concerns as Members of Congress. But to do that is going to require some major infrastructure questions because you cannot say we are for fastpass and not have enough lanes. And physically we have rivers in some of these borders and this is a very costly proposition.

Mr. Cummings.

Mr. CUMMINGS. Thank you very much, Mr. Chairman. And Ms. Tischler, thank you very much for being here.

I agree with the chairman that the Customs unquestionably has a very difficult challenge. And consistent with that, I guess we have a lot of people who are working overtime now?

Ms. TISCHLER. Yes, sir.

Mr. CUMMINGS. And what are we doing about bringing in new people?

Ms. TISCHLER. Well, we have been very fortunate this year, thanks to Congress and the administration for supporting efforts to increase our rolls. Just in the 2000 arena, that is all I can speak to, we almost have gone up about 1,000 people. And it is split between the Customs inspectors, as I pointed out before, the K–9 officers and our agents. So the total number of inspectors that we are getting actually as a result of the 2002 initiatives and the supplemental is 919. And the total number of agents is 381. And we are quite happy about that. We have been pretty static for the last number of years. It was pretty hard to spread people around. In fact in 1999, when the Rasson incident happened and we had to send people to the border, then we realized exactly how thin we were on the Northern border. That is why a lot of these individuals are going to be reporting to the Northern border ports.

Mr. CUMMINGS. One of the things that was very interesting during one of our hearings that—we were talking about—the issue of airline security came up. And it may have actually been in another committee that I am on. And they were saying that—how as they had to get more of these folks that ride in the airplanes, the security.

Ms. TISCHLER. Sky marshals.

Mr. CUMMINGS. Sky marshals. That—so many new terms here. I asked them where were these people coming from, the new people. And they said most of them were coming from the Border Patrol, which is very interesting. I am just wondering where are your people coming from? Is there any particular place that you see a high number of them coming?

Ms. TISCHLER. We have lost a few to TSA as well in their endeavor to staff the sky marshal area. When we are recruiting, we recruit in the widest area possible. And so, frankly, does INS. So it sort of depends on who actually puts in. But we just had a team, for instance, in New England looking to staff the Northern border because we realize it is possible that if you hire somebody from the southwest border and try to send them to Beecher Falls, they might not stay there too long. So we try very diligently to fit the right person with the right job.

And we are recruiting all across the United States right now. So we do not expect really to pull from the other agencies except for the special agent position.

Mr. CUMMINGS. Not very long ago I got a call I think from The New York Times, and they were trying to pull together an article about how since September 11th there had been an increase in the amount of drugs that have been found by Customs and they wanted me to comment.

And is that accurate, first of all? Have we seen an increase in drug discoveries?

Ms. TISCHLER. Customs has—we have just recently run a survey on that, and it appears to us that we have been able to interdict a lot more drugs coming across the southwest border, and even coming across the Northern border. Although it is pretty restricted to certain areas. So we would agree with that.

Mr. CUMMINGS. And is that because the surveillance is much stricter?

Ms. TISCHLER. I would like to think it is a function of the number of people up there, yeah.

Mr. CUMMINGS. And as far as going back for a moment to the new peopling coming in, is the training that they receive now much different than it was say pre-September 11th?

Ms. TISCHLER. No. Our training has really been pretty consistent over the years. Like I said, the issue of how to address smuggling on the border or how to address how to process commercial traffic pretty well stays the same. What we have added is a new focus on terrorist activities. How to spot anomalies that might lead us in that direction. I am not being facetious, but what a weapon of mass destruction might look like, how to work the radiation pagers, how to deal with some of the new technology that we are going to be using to look for chemicals that are inbound.

So, in general, training really hasn't changed that much in specific. To deal with the area of terrorism, we pretty well are cranking up our program to include new areas that will impact on that.

Mr. CUMMINGS. Just one other question. And I would be more than remiss if I did not ask you this. I do not think I could go back to my district. You know, there was a time, and it is a little unrelated but related, about a year or so ago when African-Americans were very concerned that the Customs, particularly airlines, we would be having all kind of problems. African-American women were disproportionately being checked at the airports. And I know that—I guess that may have been about 2 years ago. Our colleague, John Lewis, spoke out against it at the Congressional Black Caucus. And African-American men were being disproportionately stopped and checked and searched, in many instances strip-searched. And I was just wondering has a—I know that back then some new policies were put in place.

And I was just wondering how those policies were working out? I know this is a little unrelated, but I have to ask you since I have you here before us.

Ms. TISCHLER. Even prior to September 11th, the level of noise, the level of complaints, letters we were getting in had completely fallen off. So we are very pleased with the policies that we put into place. Our training on personal search has proven to be really reliable.

Our search efficiency rate, meaning the numbers of people searched and what we actually find on them, has actually gone up. Because, for instance, in one of our ports, I will not tell you which, they searched like 1,000 people and got very little return. Well, they have searched a lot fewer people than the 1,000 people within that same timeframe and their search efficiency rate went way up. They have made seizures where none existed before.

So Customs has really taken a lot of time, energy, and put a lot of money behind straightening that perceived problem out. And we are pleased.

Mr. CUMMINGS. Thank you very much.

Mr. SOUDER. Our economy in Indiana would die if we were restricted much with our Canadian trade because it has become a huge part because of NAFTA, in addition to trade with Mexico. So we are very concerned how to keep the commerce moving, particularly if we have additional terrorist incidents, which we know at some point we will have in the United States, and how our country is going to a react on the borders. Since September 11th it has gone down to near manageable levels again, and we have done that with a lot of stress. We are bringing in the systems. But we all know that this isn't a problem that is suddenly over, and therefore we are likely to see the pressures.

We all know that this expedited clearance process is critical. So I have some very specific questions related to this. One pilot program which is a joint venture between Customs and the State of New Hampshire apparently will involve a Slovakian factory and a U.S. importer. The goods will be inspected and sealed at the factory in Slovakia and then brought into the United States. Who will carry out the inspections at the point of origin? Will the U.S. Customs do that? Will they simply supervise them? If it is the latter, will the private firms that make or carry the goods be entrusted with the inspections or will the foreign nations' customs inspectors carry them out?

In other words, how is this process exactly going to work? Because this is vital in the preclearance questions and in the security question.

Ms. TISCHLER. Correct. The Croatian pilot is Operation Safeguard. It is being sponsored by the Coast Guard. I believe they are going to be handling the security issues overseas.

But let me say this, that the concept of what Safeguard is trying to pilot, the issue of a company securing its supply chain from start to when it gets to American Customs, is an apt one. That is what that CTPAT concept and CSI, the Container Security Initiative, is all about, In Canada, however, which is something I can speak to, we have got inspectors at Vancouver, Montreal and Halifax. We are cooperating with our Canadian counterparts. We do the targeting with them. We are showing them how to do it as well.

By the way, they have got people now at Seattle and Newark that are doing the same things for cargo going to Canada.

But once we identify an anomaly, we set the container to the side. They are handling it. The Canadians are handling it, with us observing. They are running these containers through NII that they have got, and/or opening the cargo. I guess I think it is fortunate that we have come up with nothing. But we have done a number of containers. We just sent our inspectors into Halifax and Montreal the week before last. So we know what is going to happen there.

The idea is, I know—I do not think I am speaking out of turn if I tell you, we have already been to one of the mega ports and have been negotiating with this country—I really do not want to say what it is, because I don't want to put them on the spot. But they seem very receptive of the idea of us sending inspectors over there again to target.

Now in terms of who is going do the searching and what they are going to do with the stuff if we do interdict something, from a law enforcement perspective in the context of narcotics, will we try to do a controlled delivery? Will they handle it there? That all remains to be seen. I think as we go to each country that has one of those mega ports or even beyond that, it is going to be a function of how we deal with that country and what law enforcement is available there, what kind of NII they actually have.

I know we have been talking to the State Department about the possibility of providing NII to some of these ports that don't have anything. It just makes sense to do that. But I do have to say that there are some bills before Congress right now which would help us out, absent that, and even including that. And that is a House bill and a Senate bill that speak to reforming the way we look at the manifests and trying to get them far in advance.

We would like to see an electronic transfer of manifest information. We would like more detailed and accurate manifest information and we would like it 24 hours before a ship, for instance, would depart from a port overseas. I think some of the proposals have revolved around 5 days which works pretty well for Europe and Asia, but for this hemisphere it doesn't work very well when this stuff is coming in from Grand Bahama Island which is hours away from Miami. So we are looking for a little tinkering with the bills.

But back to overseas. So far the countries that we have talked to have been receptive. And I think, as they say, the devil is in the details.

Mr. SOUDER. Will your ACE computer system be able to handle all of this data?

Ms. TISCHLER. When ACE finally gets up and running, absolutely. ACS is going to be a little stretched.

Mr. SOUDER. Would it be—a little stretched means it might not be able to handle it?

Ms. TISCHLER. I think for the short term, within the next couple of years, it will be able to handle it fine. It is just that it is not as sophisticated as we would like to do data analysis and trend analysis. And it is in that area where the information would come in and then be used to, in fact, target cargo that will be a little on the lacking side. That is why we are so anxious to get ACE up and running.

Mr. SOUDER. I know the president of Mexico has taken tremendous strides in cleaning up a lot of the corruption in Mexico but it is a prevalent problem in their police departments. And one of the problems in the south border is we are dependent on their local police commanders because there is no central criminal data base. I would suggest that this probably presents problems on rail and other things coming in, not only with Mexico but other countries. Would you agree with that statement?

Ms. TISCHLER. I am not knowledgeable enough to actually agree with you. But I would say that would present a problem, if true. I know that Mexican Customs is investing pretty heavily in IT, and they feel that they are going to be very sophisticated in order to interface with ACE, and our Canadian partners as well.

Mr. SOUDER. In your reference to the legislation, I think it is fair to say, that much like we did on the airline manifests and have put pressure on the different countries to provide us with the names of the people heading into this country, to make the fastpass systems work, whether they are NEXUS or SENTRI or whatever types of preclearances, we are going to have to have more data.

Now I know trucking companies and others and shippers are going to want to add things at the last minute. That is the nature of the business. But to the degree you do that, we don't have the same sense of security. One of the things that we have raised at some of our hearings with some Canadian trucking companies, at one of the hearings with others, is that probably there are going to need to be more severe penalties if you abuse the preclearance system, because the—the integrity of that system is vital to the movement of commerce. And it is almost like having a specially vetted unit. When you ask for special privileges, which we need to do, we need to have special obligations, clearances to make sure that this doesn't become a prime target to slip contraband and terrorists through. And we are certainly going to make sure that these type of things are there. But we also have to make sure that you have got the technology and the computers, because it doesn't do us any good to set up a system if you can't get the data in.

One last question on that. There have been proposals to put GPS transponders on cargo. I assume that the current system wouldn't handle that. Would ACE be able to have the capacity to handle that?

Ms. TISCHLER. Yes. But I have to tell you that we were—in fact, Mr. Koch, who is on your next panel, and I were speaking about this very thing this morning. There are a number of vendors out there that are talking to Customs and Transportation about what would constitute a smart container and how you would in fact track inventory around. Just yesterday a vendor came in to talk to us about it and I actually gave him Mr. Koch's name and phone number because we would like to pilot something like that soon. And it is just a function of what it is.

We understand that the Department of Defense might have had a system they used, and are still using, actually, but they developed it during the Gulf War to track their ammunition and munitions around. So if that is true, then it would be something that would be very helpful. But we could not handle this unless our partners agreed to some type of test.

Mr. SOUDER. These are difficult questions. We rode in to the LA Harbor with some of the sea marshals, which meant boarding a ship at 4 something in the morning. It was moving a little faster than I thought it was going to be when—it didn't look like we were moving until you get ready to step across that—being a landlubber.

But one of the things that is apparent—and this particular one, it was a cruise ship. But in these ships that, even if you have the integrity of the system at the point of origin, in the—and we are checking it, at least partially as they come in, we also have to have some assurance in the transshipment process that something isn't altered or added. And many of these flags that the ships are coming in under are questionable.

And that—and that, even in the cruise ship that we boarded, it was very noticeable as we went through with the people from INS and Customs and down into the underbelly of the ship and talked to the people who were actually controlling it, they were up with the harbor pilot much like the sky marshals do as they enter the closeness of the harbor, but on top of that, the—the operating crew not only didn't speak English, they spoke a multitude of languages. And that is why this other—these other questions of tracking the cargo inside become critical.

And it isn't that we have to do every piece, but we need to make enough uncertainty and enough accountability that the American public has confidence. Because, like I mentioned before, September 11th, none of us knew it was coming. Our level of accountability in Congress and the government and the potential reaction if we have further problems is going to be so out of proportion to what the reaction was even in September 11th, that we are preparing over a period of a number of years in our computer systems, our infrastructure. And I hope you are looking at all of those interrelationships. Because we want to make the commerce work. And we need to know from you where the problems are and what the actual resource costs are that we have to look at here in Congress when we make these abstract decisions that sound good, and then tell you to go do it and don't give you the money.

Ms. TISCHLER. That is correct. And, in truth, it is an unknown universe right now. That is why it is so important to partner with the trade. Because they have got a piece of the puzzle. Transportation—I don't mean the department, I mean the trade portion of transportation has in fact used some of this technology over the years. We put a technology subcommittee together under CTPAT to explore all of the technology that the different transportation universes were using, sea, land, air, rail. It is amazing because they didn't know pretty much about what each other were using, which meant there is a lot of duplication of effort.

And so part of CTPAT is trying to avoid the duplication and turn everybody on to technology. That seems to be the best practice.

Mr. SOUDER. Thank you. Mr. Cummings, do you have additional questions?

Mr. CUMMINGS. Just a few other questions.

You briefly mentioned Operation Green Quest. Would you talk about that a little further, please.

Ms. TISCHLER. Operation Green Quest is an antiterrorism money-laundering operation that Customs, Treasury and the Justice agencies stood up in October, to really get at the soft underbelly, if you will, of terrorism.

I personally—I have been in law enforcement for almost 31 years now, and I have watched us try to interdict narcotics and do narcotics investigations. But my background is money-laundering. And I am a firm believer in taking the money out of the equation. And so what Green Quest was designed to do basically was trace and track illicit funds or licit funds that were in fact being used for terrorist purposes.

Mr. CUMMINGS. It was interesting that—the other day one of the Cabinet members over there in Afghanistan made a—made a speech about trying to make sure that, you know, illegal drugs would be stopped and the growing of various crops leading to the distribution of illegal drugs. And I was just wondering, if it is not too confidential, are we looking at Afghanistan?

Ms. TISCHLER. We have always looked at Afghanistan because of the heroin trade. Similar to what has happened with Columbia with the FARC, the cocaine traffic has fueled the FARC down there. And we know darn well that the heroin trade has been fueling bin Laden and others who would seek to destroy our way of life.

So we have been actually dealing with it from a narcotics illicit proceeds perspective for some time now.

Mr. CUMMINGS. Uh-huh. And are we—does this—has Customs at all worked with the government of Afghanistan, giving advice or anything of that nature, to your knowledge?

Ms. TISCHLER. Up to now? No.

Mr. CUMMINGS. You mentioned that the Customs, Department of Transportation working group presented a report to the Office of Homeland Security making recommendations to improve container security. Is that report available publicly?

Ms. TISCHLER. I don't know if it has actually gone to the coordination committee PCC or not. I know that it was due to go. Then they were going to review it and open it up for review.

Mr. CUMMINGS. And so the next step is opening it up for review? It has several recommendations?

Ms. TISCHLER. It has a number of recommendations. I think there are 25 recommendations.

Mr. CUMMINGS. And I take it that the Office of Homeland Security would have a lot to do with making sure that those recommendations, the ones that they felt appropriate, went into effect. Is that accurate?

Ms. TISCHLER. I think that they are submitting it to them for their thoughts. Some of the recommendations will require funding. I am sure that we will have to take it to Congress to discuss these recommendations.

Homeland security, I think, will spearpoint these recommendations once they finish looking at the report and digesting the elements.

Mr. CUMMINGS. Mr. Chairman, I yield the balance of my time to Congressman Davis, if you had any questions.

Mr. SOUDER. Mr. Davis will get 5 minutes plus any additional.

Mr. DAVIS. Thank you very much, Mr. Chairman. I want to thank the gentleman for yielding. I also want to thank you and commend you, both you and Representative Cummings, for the diligence with which you have pursued this whole issue and the diligence that you are taking to look at the whole question of drug trafficking, the whole business of crime, criminality and even looking at the whole question of prevention and how we can really get a handle on drug policy that is effective for our country.

I also want to thank you for your testimony. I have enjoyed listening to your responses. The questions that sort of come to mind in terms of border effectiveness obviously require a great deal of cooperation between countries. What are our experiences right now in terms of the level of cooperation that we are receiving from other countries with whom we have to interact at the borders?

Ms. TISCHLER. Well, I would like to talk about Canada. We have always cooperated with Canadian Customs and vice versa. And we deal with the RCMP, frankly, on a recurring basis. The Smart Border Accord that our two countries have struck, I think, will go a long way to increasing that cooperation.

We have the same focus, how to keep terrorists out of the United States and possibly out of Canada and still have that trade go through which is so critical to the border areas.

So I've got nothing but pluses for the Canadians. And we have recently started the same type of proposed accord with Mexico. I think President Fox has gone a long way to straightening things out in Mexico. And we've always dealt the same thing with Mexican customs on a very positive level. They've recently within the last couple of years, they have a whole new cast of managers that are managing Mexican customs. We have been dealing with them in enforcement and working groups that have to do with the trade. Things have been coming along quite well as far as we are concerned.

As far as our counterparts overseas, we deal extremely well with the British, the French, the Germans. In Asia, our cooperative efforts extend to Thailand and Singapore. And we just opened an office actually in India.

I really truly believe in a global trade environment, Customs has got to be able to maintain positive relationships with not only our counterparts but their government as well. And so far over the years, it's worked out quite well. There is a World Customs Organization, actually, where all the countries come together with Customs and we deal quite a bit with them as well as with the Interpol to really establish and keep up these cooperative efforts.

Mr. DAVIS. As we increase reliance upon technology, and as there are continuing advances in technological development, are we still getting the human person power, I mean, the reliance obviously upon the expertise of agents, of humans who work in the process? Are we getting what we need in terms of interest and in terms of people being interested in entering the service?

Ms. TISCHLER. We think so. Customs relies on a tiered-up process, anyway. We have lines of defense. For instance, in narcotics we have inspectors, we have our dog handlers with our canines, of course, and the NII, the technology all working in concert with each other. And so now that we are expanding, we are fortunate enough to get a number of personnel resources committed off the 2002 supplemental and the initiatives, and we are recruiting for an individual that has—of course, not too hard with these kids these days because they are much better at computers than I ever was, that's for sure—but we are looking for people with specific interests. Language capabilities, multicultural issues come into play here. So we are trying to draw from a very broad segment of the population in order to do the best customer service in law enforcement that we can.

Mr. DAVIS. Representative Meeks and I spent a great deal of time working with Commissioner Kelly during the past administration and we saw some of the new processes and procedures that were being put into place designed to cut down on the number of complaints relative to the issue of profiling and the concerns that Representative Cummings expressed a little bit about. Are we finding that the new technology, the screening devices, for example, that were put in, have they reduced significantly, to your knowledge, the number of complaints about strip-searching and profiling and that kind of issue?

Ms. TISCHLER. I had been explaining previously the level of our complaints as well is way down. Way down. I couldn't point specifically to technology. I would like to think it was our training and our—and in the bicultural areas that we have been doing and our personal search training and the levels of review that have to be undertaken before somebody can, in fact, search someone bodily. That is actually contributing to that. Our body scan machines have been useful, but they are on a voluntary basis and most people who are faced with a search actually decline them. They would rather be hand-searched.

Mr. DAVIS. And so you are monitoring that aspect of the new developments closely so that we know that there is, in fact, adherence to the new policies and procedures? I mean that's a real part, I would assume.

Ms. TISCHLER. Yes, sir, it's part of our internal control system.

Mr. DAVIS. Well, let me commend you in terms of—I mean, I think there have indeed been improvements in that arena. Obviously, we are never out of the water. We've never done as well as we can do. I think we are always becoming. But I certainly have not received the number of complaints that I was getting, you know, coming out of the area where I live and spent a great deal of my time in Chicago, where there is a tremendous amount of traffic. And so I certainly want to commend you and commend the agency for progress in that arena.

I have no other questions, Mr. Chairman. And thank you very much.

Mr. SOUDER. Thank you, Mr. Davis. And thank you, Ms. Tischler, for your testimony today. We'll have some additional written questions, but it was very helpful as we look at some of these complex matters. And please accept on behalf of the Customs department our sincere thanks for all the hard work in the field from the many agents who have worked overtime and who have been so steadfast.

In Port Angeles, we went over and met with Diana Dean, and you made a reference earlier to the individual experience and skill of the customs officer on the ground. So much of this is instinct, and that with people who see something a little different on the bottom of one truck and lead to a huge bust.

Even with all the technology, it's also the agents in the field. And we need to make sure they have the best technology, but we also need the experience in the training. Thank you very much for being here today.

Ms. TISCHLER. Thank you, sir.

Mr. SOUDER. If the second panel could now come forward. Mr. Larry Johnson, Ms. Colleen Kelley, Mr. T.J. Bonner, Mr. Christopher Koch, Mr. John Simpson, and Mr. Steve Russell.

We will wait until you all get seated and then we will ask you to stand up.

If you could each stand and raise your right hand. It is our customary procedure as an oversight committee to swear in each witness.

[Witnesses sworn.]

Mr. SOUDER. Let the record show that all the witnesses responded in the affirmative. You have now joined in this distinguished room—this is the committee that has done everything from the travel office to the China investigations to Waco and oversight investigations since—for a number of years since we have taken over. And it's our customary procedure to do that.

Your testimony today, even though it's for many of you a long way to travel for 5 minutes, and with the questions, this is building a systematic hearing record on border security in particular and the interrelationship of Congress, INS and security that isn't matched anywhere else in the system. Because we have been doing field hearings in the North, field hearings in the South. I have had all the commissioners in from the different agencies and we want to make sure here in Washington that we hear from the business side as well. These are huge questions, as we look at the multiple missions of these agencies. And if we throw them together, how is that going to impact our trade and our security efforts?

So I thank each of you for taking this time today and being part of our efforts to sort this through. We will begin with Mr. Johnson, a very frequent witness over the years to this committee, as we have dealt with—this subcommittee in particular as we have dealt with counterterrorism questions long before the whole world was focused on counterterrorism. We appreciate your tremendous insights.

STATEMENTS OF LARRY C. JOHNSON, CEO AND FOUNDER, BERG ASSOCIATES LLC; COLLEEN M. KELLEY, NATIONAL PRESIDENT, NATIONAL TREASURY EMPLOYEES UNION; T.J. BONNER, PRESIDENT, NATIONAL BORDER PATROL COUNCIL, AMERICAN FEDERATION OF GOVERNMENT EMPLOYEES; CHRISTOPHER KOCH, PRESIDENT, WORLD SHIPPING COUNCIL; JOHN SIMPSON, PRESIDENT, AMERICAN ASSOCIATION OF EXPORTERS AND IMPORTERS; AND STEVE RUSSELL, CHAIRMAN AND CEO, CELADON TRUCKING SERVICES, AMERICAN TRUCKING ASSOCIATIONS

Mr. JOHNSON. Thank you, Congressman Souder. It's a privilege to be with you again today. I ask that my full statement be made a part of the record. Over the last 3 years, in my company and current business, we spent a lot of time in Latin America, and specifically in the Colon Free Zone of Panama, doing undercover operations and tracking product counterfeiting. In the course of doing that, we have gotten some insights that address this whole issue of both border security, port security and some gaps that need to be closed, and in my statement I outline what I think are five broad areas that need to be addressed.

One of those in particular is the need for clearinghouse with the whole security technology R&D. Right now the U.S. Government is spending a lot of money in a lot of different arenas in a lot of different agencies trying to develop technology. But at the end of the day there is no one place that is helping sort out and establish priorities.

So, for example, a lot of what is now the TSA center up in New Jersey, there is efforts to develop explosive detection systems, separate efforts to develop cargo systems. This much I know: The U.S. Government and the people of the United States have an enormous talent and scientific ability, and when you put that together with the talents that are resident in the national laboratories, it is beyond me why we have not been able to harness all of that into a concentrated, if you will, Manhattan effort to develop effective security technology. Because there is a legitimate question here about you don't want to stop commerce by unnecessary inspections, but there are ways to develop that technology. The key for it is money has to be appropriated. We saw this with the explosive detection systems. It was recommended back in 1990 after Pan Am 103 to do it, but Congress and the administrations, both Republican and Democrat, never appropriated the money to put those machines and get them out and create a market for it until after September 11th. And we cannot wait until we have a disaster in a port to do that.

A second issue—and I endorse the concept of putting INS and Customs and Coast Guard together in some fashion. And I think if I had to weigh in on one side, I think it would be better to bring INS and Coast Guard under Customs as opposed to subjecting others to the Department of Justice.

But right now when you have three different chiefs directing things, that means nobody is in charge and at the end of the day there is a great need for coordination in this front.

And I outline in my testimony the problem of stovepiping of information. Not just keeping information within the Federal agencies, where DEA doesn't talk to Customs and doesn't talk to FBI, and there is not a flow of information across that direction, but you also see in my testimony an e-mail I received from a law enforcement officer in the United States who worked out in the West Coast near a U.S. military base, and he recounts his frustrations of making repeated efforts first to alert the FBI to what he thought was a Middle Eastern cell operating near this military base that handles nuclear weapons. And the FBI said—and this was 3 years ago—we're not doing profiling and we're not going to focus on it.

He has subsequently gone back to them because he has identified some activities that relate to Hispanics and the FBI said, no, no, we are focused only on the Middle Eastern side.

What you have here is a law enforcement officer who is extremely frustrated with what he sees as the inability of Federal officials to receive the information that State and local cops have, as well as for the State and local cops to get that information where they can be a part of the national security effort.

The last point I'll make—and I intended to bring a Power Point presentation for you today, and I admit that I did not know how to properly use zip files so I sent the wrong one—but it illustrates the problem of visas and making sure that we go after these overseas in the right way.

Now the picture I was going to show you was one of Walid Zayed Massis. Mr. Zayed, I ran across in the course of doing an investigation in product counterfeiting. What made him even more interesting after we got him on this charge was he was the first individual convicted in Panama for money-laundering. But in 1989 he published a book that its English translation is "Palestine: The Burning Silence." He also happens to be the intelligence chief for the PLO in Central and South America and is on the record calling for the extinction of Israel. He is involved and has links to groups and individuals that are involved in terrorism.

This individual also happens to have a company that is incorporated in the United States. Now when you look at U.S. visa law, there is nothing in U.S. visa law, because he has not been convicted of drug trafficking, and because the only other category for excluding him on is this vague thing called moral turpitude, we have made efforts in the course of our business to get people like Mr. Zayed blocked from getting visas to come to the United States.

In another instance, we ran across an individual who was not engaged in terrorism, but was using his trips to the United States every year to go to U.S. companies' marketplace, identify the new products, take pictures, go back home, place an order in China, and then the Chinese would manufacture these counterfeit items that he would then bring in. He had been convicted in Venezuela. It has gone all the way to the Supreme Court. The conviction has been upheld. But despite that conviction, when we went to the U.S. Embassy and said block this individual from coming into the United States and using the United States as a tool for attacking U.S. companies, the U.S. Embassy said under visa law we cannot stop him. Product counterfeiting is not moral turpitude.

Now those kinds of gaps I find completely senseless. I mean, this is a place where we need to have common sense come into the picture. We don't want to block people who have a legitimate desire to come to the United States. But the individuals who are engaged with the criminal activity, the drug trafficking, the money-laundering, and potentially terrorism, it is a small group of people. But in my experience, they have been very effective exploiting the loopholes that exist in both U.S. ports of entry and in U.S. law.

[The prepared statement of Mr. Johnson follows:]

TESTIMONY OF LARRY C. JOHNSON BEFORE THE SUBCOMMITTE ON CRIMINAL JUSTICE, DRUG POLICY, AND HUMAN RESOURCES
10 April 2002

I appreciate the opportunity to address this Committee on the issue of what can be done to improve security and efficiency at our nation's borders and ports of entry. While the focus of our nation remains on the threat of terrorism, we should expand our vision towards a more complete approach to security. In other words, if we deploy technology at ports of entry designed to detect explosives we also may detect illegal drugs, money from drug proceeds or contraband. Effective security measures and technology work to defeat and deter a wide range of threats.

Everyone wants secure borders but there is no consensus within the U.S. Government on what constitutes secure borders. Before we can design and deploy security technologies there must be some agreement on the exact objectives we are trying to achieve. At a minimum I believe we should strive to achieve three objectives:

1. **Ensuring that law enforcement officials at borders and ports of entry can quickly and efficiently verify the identity of people and check them against relevant databases.**
2. **Screening all containers bringing goods into the United States to ensure that undeclared items that could create a hazard are not being covertly introduced into the country.**
3. **Ensuring that state and local law enforcement officials have access to information that will enable them to apprehend individuals who have entered the United States illegally or who have overstayed their visas.**

These "simple" goals are not easily obtained. We can close the vulnerabilities we face on our borders and at ports of entry only through a coordinated, integrated strategy that simultaneously addresses the issues of technology, bureaucratic lines of authority, and immigration law. In terms of practical steps Congress should consider:

- **Putting all U.S. Government technical R&D under one authority.**
- **Authorizing and appropriating sufficient funds to develop and deploy security technology.**
- **Consolidating the capabilities of INS, U.S. Customs, and the Coast Guard under one chain of command.**
- **Eliminating the stove piping among agencies with respect to the sharing of immigration information and enforcement activities.**
- **Changing US immigration law to exclude foreigners convicted of felonies.**

We need a security detection R&D clearinghouse. At present the U.S. Government is pursuing a variety of security detection technology R&D efforts. Some of the work is being done at the TSA Tech Center. Some is being done within the National Laboratories. Some is being carried out under the auspices of the Counter Terrorism Technical Scientific

Working Group. And still other work is being carried out in the private sector. While I have not had time to do a complete survey of who is doing what I have spoken with key people in the Executive Branch and with GAO who all agree that there is no coherent comprehensive vision.

While a security technology clearinghouse can provide Congress with a clear roadmap of the technology that needs to be developed, Congress must take the lead in ensuring that the required funds for developing the technology is appropriated. I was working at State Department in the Office of Counter Terrorism in 1990 when the President's Commission on Pan Am 103 issued its report. One of the key findings in that report called for developing and deploying explosive detection systems at US airports. Notwithstanding this requirement, neither the administration of President George H.W. Bush or President William J. Clinton provided the necessary funds to get the technology fully developed and deployed. Without the intervention of the US Government there was not a sufficient demand in the private sector to create a viable market to attract manufacturers. It was only in the wake of the terrorist attacks of September 11th that the US Congress and the Executive Branch finally decided to act to address this deficiency. My intent is not to look backward and try to assign blame; instead, I bring up the past in hopes we will learn from our past mistakes. At the end of the day, the Congress must lead in appropriating funds to produce the necessary security technology and in holding the Executive Branch's feet to the fire.

Streamlining the chains of command for border and port security must also be a priority. The men and women currently working for US Customs, INS, and the Coast Guard are hardworking, patriotic Americans who want to do the right thing. But in carrying out their daily responsibilities they work for three separate chiefs—the Secretary of Treasury, the Attorney General, and the Secretary of Transportation. While the President exercises the ultimate legal authority the day-to-day reality finds these agencies working, under the best of circumstances, independently, and under the worst case, at cross purposes. I am not familiar with all of the proposals being floated for consolidating these various functions but I am certain that at the end of the day we need one person ultimately in charge and accountable for securing the borders and the ports of entry. The essence of this authority is that someone is empowered to provide the President with a coordinated plan for securing the borders and ports and, once given the funds, is held accountable for carrying out the mission.

Getting the various Federal bureaucracies with border and port security to work together is only the first step. We must also ensure that the immigration and customs information that is stored in a variety of discrete databases is integrated into a system that is accessible to Federal law enforcement as well as state and local police. Following one of my recent television appearances to discuss security matters I received an email from a policeman out west. His concerns are self-explanatory:

> *In 1998 I had several Middle East players under Surveillance. They operated in groups of four, together in one vehicle with another subject following in a chase vehicle. They were making contact with a subject from a Communist Country. This was three blocks from a Military Installation. Because I kept track of U.S. State Department briefings about terrorist activity I considered their activity suspicious and called the FBI and ran it*

by them. The Agent told me that he was not allowed to "Profile" anyone. I expressed my concern about possible terrorist activity by Middle East players. He told me he was more concerned about the Russians.

I continued my surveillance and continued to call the FBI with License Numbers and descriptions. This group made several contacts over two years until RESSAM was arrested in Port Angeles with 100 lbs of explosive (December 1999). Right after that this group had the largest meeting I had seen in two years. After that they never made contact again. I have not seen the Middle East players around town since then.

This month I informed the Bureau that a large group of Latinos was meeting at a park two blocks from a strategic U.S. military base. The agent told me the Bureau wasn't interested in Hispanics/Latinos and he doubted the INS was either because they were focused on Middle East Players. This group is all in their 20's, military age, extremely fit, numbering about 30-40. I reminded the Bureau there are many other cells out there besides Al Qaeda. He said and they are all being ignored right now (sic).

Unfortunately this is not the view of one disgruntled individual. This is a good cop who works at the local level and wants to help protect the United States. I have heard the same complaint from other officers across the United States. Simply put, we need to make sure that our State and Local police get a receptive ear when they try to help out Federal Officials and that they have access to information gathered by the Feds that will enable them to do a better job.

Finally, there is the issue of who gets a visa to come to this country. There is a link between people who engage in money laundering or drug trafficking and terrorism. The attached power point presentation highlights the case of Mr. Walid Zayed Massis. Mr. Zayed is a merchant in the Colon Free Zone of Panama. He was the first case of money laundering prosecuted in Panama. I came across Mr. Zayed during an investigation into product counterfeiting. When we raided his warehouse in the Colon Free Zone of Panama I learned that Mr. Zayed was involved in more than product counterfeiting. He also is a close associate of Yassir Arafat and is cited in the press as the head of the Intifada for Central and South America. Mr. Zayed's book, PALESTINE: THE BURNING SILENCE, makes clear his sympathies with groups that engage in terrorist attacks against Israel and his support of policies to eliminate Israel as a nation. If Mr. Zayed had not been convicted of money laundering in Panama he would be entitled to a visa to the United States. I believe that people who endorse or support groups that engage in terrorism should not enjoy the privilege of visiting or living in the United States.

I encourage the Congress to take a new look at 8 USCS § 1182, which allows for a visa denial only if a person is guilty of moral turpitude or drug trafficking. A person who has committed murder is not necessarily precluded from visiting the United States. I was involved recently in product counterfeiting case in Venezuela. A Caracas-based merchant traveled every year to the United States for a trade show where he saw the latest products of a US company. The individual returned home and commissioned manufacturers in China to make an exact copy of the product. Although this merchant was convicted in Venezuela of counterfeiting the US Embassy in Caracas declined to lift his visa. Under current U.S. law people who are felons can still get a visa to the United States. We need to

give U.S. consular officials clearer instructions and more power to prevent criminals and felons from coming to the United States.

Perfect security is an unrealistic goal. However, sound security is within our reach. I believe the objectives and proposals I have outlined today will over the long run enhance our security as a nation without jeopardizing the freedoms we cherish.

Mr. SOUDER. Well, thank you for that fairly discouraging testimony.

Mr. JOHNSON. Sorry about that.

Mr. SOUDER. And if you would like to submit the other power points for the record.

Mr. JOHNSON. I will get that to you and will figure out how to use it properly.

Mr. SOUDER. Thank you very much, Mr. Chairman. Ms. Kelley, you are next.

Ms. KELLEY. Thank you, Chairman Souder, Ranking Member Cummings. I appreciate the subcommittee holding this hearing today and having the opportunity to testify on the enhancement of border and port-of-entry security. As the president of NTEU, I have the honor of leading a union which represents over 12,000 Customs employees across the country. Customs inspectors and canine enforcement officers make up our Nation's first line of defense in the wars on terrorism, on drugs, and on illegal contraband.

The U.S. Customs Service continues to be the Nation's premier border agency by interdicting more drugs than any other agency. Customs is also a revenue collection agency, collecting an estimated $25 billion in revenue each year on over 25 million entries involving $1.3 trillion in international trade every year.

One of the most discussed ideas being debated on the topic of border and port-of-entry security is the idea of border agency consolidation. And the most talked about border agency consolidation proposal, although we have not yet seen one from the administration, would combine the Customs Service, INS and the Border Patrol into one agency under the jurisdiction of the Department of Justice.

I find this proposal to be extremely troubling. Unfortunately, this type of a border agency consolidation plan would not improve but, in fact, exacerbate current border problems. The management of the Justice Department and its recent highly visible errors indicate that the lack of a sound organizational structure with regard to the border security agencies currently under its jurisdiction needs to be looked at very carefully.

Consolidating these three organizations would take attention away from critical homeland security priorities. Each one of these agencies' missions is very unique and it should remain within their current agency structure. Ignoring each agency's field of expertise will lead to losing the expertise that agency currently possesses.

Customs personnel expertise include using advanced manifest information on goods to improve targeting systems to detect questionable shipments as well as deploying state-of-the-art inspection technology and advanced computer systems at land borders, at airports and at seaports.

Another popular argument in favor of consolidation involves the perceived lack of intelligence-sharing between border security agencies. Since September 11th, Customs and INS receive FBI intelligence briefings. These briefings should have been happening on a regular basis even before September 11th. But these briefings demonstrate that consolidation isn't necessary to improve intelligence-sharing. There are other ways to do it and there needs to be other ways to do it.

In Customs' case, no one doubts that the level of conveyances of cargo and of passengers has increased dramatically, but unfortunately, its resources have not kept pace. In fact, Customs' internal review of staffing done over a year ago, which they call the resource allocation model or RAM, shows that Customs needs over 14,000 additional positions just to fill its basic mission, and that was before September 11th.

For instance, with increased funding, modern technologies such as the VACIS, which is the vehicle and cargo inspection systems, could be acquired. However, adequate and consistent funding to purchase, to operate, and to maintain these technologies has not been forthcoming. The President's fiscal year 2003 budget requests a token increase from last year's appropriations and is simply inadequate to meet the needs of the Customs personnel.

The recent deployment of over 700 unarmed National Guard troops to our borders clearly shows the need for more Customs personnel. These troops need to be removed from the borders and quickly replaced with highly trained Customs personnel.

Last year, Congress acknowledged the shortage of staffing and resources by appropriating $245 million for Customs staffing and for technology, and these were included in the Department of Defense appropriations.

We urge the Congress to again increase the funds available for additional inspectors and equipment in areas around the country that are experiencing these severe shortages. The 12 and 16-hour shifts and working 6 and 7 days in a row, which Ms. Tischler testified to, cannot continue without putting the safety, the health and the effectiveness of the Customs inspectors who are doing this work at risk.

In addition to appropriations, Customs also receives funds from the COBRA user fee account. This funds all inspectional personnel overtime as well as approximately 1,100 Customs positions across the country. This account is currently at a point where there is a significant shortfall expected in fiscal year 2002. To help remedy this problem, the President's fiscal year 2003 budget proposes to temporarily increase two COBRA fees to raise an additional $250 million for personnel overtime and resource needs. Unfortunately, Congress has been extremely reluctant in the past to raise these fees, so it seems unlikely that this additional money will ever materialize. The COBRA fund is currently set to expire on September 30, 2003, unless it is reauthorized by Congress before then. COBRA must be reauthorized or Congress must appropriate additional funds to make up for the loss of these user fees in order for Customs to continue to be able to effectively deliver its mission.

I thank you again for the opportunity to testify today and look forward to any questions you might have.

[The prepared statement of Ms. Kelley follows:]

NTEU
The National Treasury Employees Union

TESTIMONY OF COLLEEN M. KELLEY
NATIONAL PRESIDENT
NATIONAL TREASURY EMPLOYEES UNION

ON

THE ENHANCMENT OF BORDER AND PORT-OF-ENTRY SECURITY

BEFORE

THE HOUSE SUBCOMMITTEE ON CRIMINAL JUSTICE, DRUG POLICY, AND HUMAN RESOURCES OF THE HOUSE GOVERNMENT REFORM COMMITTEE

WEDNESDAY, APRIL 10, 2002
2154 RAYBURN HOUSE OFFICE BUILDING
WASHINGTON, D.C.

901 E Street, N.W. • Suite 600 • Washington, D.C. 20004-2037 • (202) 783-4444

Chairman Souder, Ranking Member Cummings, distinguished members of the subcommittee, I would like to thank the Subcommittee on Criminal Justice, Drug Policy and Human Resources for the opportunity to testify on the enhancement of border and port-of-entry security.

As President of the National Treasury Employees Union (NTEU), I have the honor of leading a union which represents over 12,000 Customs employees who are stationed at 301 ports of entry across the United States. Customs inspectors and canine enforcement officers make up our nation's first line of defense in the wars on terrorism and drugs. In addition, Customs personnel are responsible for ensuring compliance with hundreds of import laws and regulations, as well as stemming the flow of illegal contraband such as child pornography, illegal arms, weapons of mass destruction and laundered money.

With a FY2002 budget of approximately $3.1 billion and over 18,500 employees, the U.S. Customs Service continues to be the Nation's premier border agency. The U.S. Customs Service interdicts more drugs than any other agency and ensures that all goods and persons entering and exiting the United States do so in compliance with over 400 U.S. laws and regulations at 301 points of entry across the country. Customs is also a revenue collection agency, collecting an estimated $25 billion in revenue on over 25 million entries involving over $1.3 trillion in international trade every year.

One of the most discussed ideas being debating on the topic of enhancing border and port-of-entry security, is the idea of border agency consolidation. The most talked about border agency consolidation proposal would combine the Customs Service, INS and the Border Patrol into one agency under the jurisdiction of the Department of Justice. I find this proposal to be extremely troubling.

One of the keys to operating any government agency is sound organization. It can ensure that problems reach their proper level of decision quickly and efficiently. More importantly, good organization helps assure accountability. Unfortunately, a border agency consolidation plan that would put the Customs Service under the jurisdiction of the Department of Justice would not improve, but exacerbate current border problems. The Justice Department has consistently shown that is has a poor record of accountability and lacks a sound organizational structure with regard to the two border security agencies currently under its jurisdiction, the INS and the Border Patrol.

Most recently, the INS notified flight schools of the approval of student visas for two of the September 11 hijackers six months after the terrorist attacks. The INS also mistakenly allowed four suspected Pakistani terrorists into the country without proper documentation and they cannot now be found. I would have to respectfully disagree with the view that consolidating the Customs Service with INS and the Border Patrol will achieve the goals of sound organization, accountability and enhanced border and port security, especially if the consolidation takes place within the Justice Department.

Consolidating these three organizations would also cause logistical and institutional chaos. It would take attention away from critical homeland security priorities. Yes, all three of these organizations deal with front line border and port security, but in very different capacities. Each of these agency's missions are unique and should remain in their current structure. Ignoring each agency's fields of expertise will lead to losing that expertise.

For example, Customs is charged with preventing contraband from entering the U.S. as well as preventing terrorists from using commercial or private transportation venues of international trade for smuggling explosives or weapons of mass destruction into or out of the United States. Customs personnel use advanced manifest information on goods to improve targeting systems to detect questionable shipments as well as deploying state of the art inspection technology at land borders, airports and seaports. Customs personnel also use advanced computer systems to compare international passenger information against law enforcement databases on a passenger-by-passenger basis to detect possible terrorists or criminals.

Whereas, the Border Patrol's primary mission is the detection and prevention of illegal entry into the United States between ports of entry, the INS is tasked with the deterrence of unlawful entry of persons into the United States as well as facilitating lawful entry of persons entering the United States at ports of entry.

The Customs Service is also responsible for collecting over $25 billion in trade revenue each year. The structure of the Department of Justice has nothing to do with revenue collection or trade facilitation, two main missions of the U.S. Customs Service. Adding revenue collection and trade facilitation responsibilities to the Department of Justice's mission would create a logistical mess and make it more difficult for U.S. companies that import and export goods.

Another popular argument in favor of consolidation involves the perceived lack of intelligence sharing between border security agencies. As any expert involved in law enforcement operations will tell you, the routine sharing of tactical intelligence is critical to all law enforcement operations, especially agencies tasked with border security. Since September 11, Customs and INS receive FBI intelligence briefings. These briefings should have happened on a regular basis before September 11, but these briefings demonstrate that consolidation isn't necessary to improve intelligence sharing.

While some work still needs to be done in the area of cooperation and coordination of intelligence, all three agencies involved with border security functions have been working together as part of Intelligence Collection and Analysis Teams (ICATs). These teams have been created throughout the country to analyze smuggling trends and concealment methods, and to quickly disseminate intelligence to all ports of entry and Border Patrol checkpoints. These ICATs are comprised of Customs Inspectors and Agents, INS agents, INS analysts and, the U.S. Border Patrol as well as local law enforcement in some cases.

In Customs' case, no one doubts that the level of conveyances, cargo and passengers has increased dramatically over the last five years, but unfortunately its resources have not kept pace. Traffic volume at U.S. land ports-of-entry has steadily increased as our shared borders with Mexico and Canada have become more open as a result of the NAFTA and other initiatives. The steady increase in non-commercial traffic has led to increased congestion and backups at many land ports-of-entry, particularly those along the Southwest border.

Nearly 68 percent of non-commercial vehicles that enter the United States entered at land ports-of-entry along the Southwest border. Wait times along the Southwest border often extend to 45 minutes or more during peak hours. Such lengthy delays can be both irritating and costly to businesses and the traveling public. The lack of resources at ports-of-entry is also a problem along the Northern Border as well as seaports. The events of September 11 brought attention to the fact that the Northern Border and the nations' seaports have long been neglected in terms of personnel and resources.

In fact, Customs recent internal review of staffing, known as the Resource Allocation Model or R.A.M. shows that Customs needed over 14,776 new hires just to fulfill its basic mission and that was before September 11. What Customs needs in order to be successful and to continue to carry out its recently expanded mission of homeland security is greater funding.

For instance, with increased funding, modern technologies, such as Vehicle and Cargo Inspection Systems (VACIS), which send gamma rays through the aluminum walls of shipping containers and vehicles to enable Customs inspectors to check for illegal drugs or weapons of mass destruction, could be acquired. However, adequate and consistent funding to purchase, operate and maintain these technologies has not been forthcoming. There have been a number of instances around the country where multi-million dollar VACIS x-ray machines have sat unused because of the lack of funding available for Customs personnel to operate the machines.

Other technologies, coupled with proper personnel funding, such as portable contraband detectors (a.k.a. Busters), optical fiber scopes and laser range finders can be invaluable to Customs personnel protecting our borders from terrorists and illegal drugs.

The President's FY2003 budget requests a funding level of $3.18 billion and 19,628 FTEs for the United States Customs Service. This request represents a token increase from last year's appropriations. NTEU feels that this budget is simply inadequate to meet the needs of Customs personnel, especially in light of the incidents surrounding September 11th.

In 2001, Customs Service employees seized over 1.7 million pounds of cocaine, heroin, marijuana and other illegal narcotics – including over 9.5 million tablets of Ecstasy, triple the amount seized in 1999. Customs also processed over 497 million travelers last year, including 1 million cars and trucks and over $1.3 trillion worth of trade. These numbers continue to grow annually. Over the last decade trade has increased by 137%. It has become very clear that funding must be substantially increased in order to allow Customs to meet the challenges of the future, especially as Customs continues to have significantly higher workloads and increased threats along America's borders.

Yet, despite the increased threats of terrorism, the dramatic increases in trade resulting from NAFTA, and new drug smuggling challenges, the Customs Service has confronted its rapidly increasing workload and homeland security mission with relatively static staffing levels and resources. In the last ten years, there have not been adequate increases in staffing levels for inspectional personnel and import specialists (the employees who process legitimate trade) to successfully conduct their missions.

The recent deployment of over 700 National Guard troops to our borders clearly shows the need for more Customs personnel. Currently, the National Guard troops are unarmed, which not only puts the Customs inspectors' lives in danger but that of the National Guard as well. In fact, a number of drug seizure cases have had to be dismissed because of the improper discovery and handling of illegal drugs by National Guard troops. These troops need to be removed from the borders and quickly replaced with highly trained Customs personnel.

Last year, Congress acknowledged the shortage of staffing and resources by appropriating $245 million for staffing and technology needs for both the Northern and Southwest Borders in the FY2001 emergency supplemental appropriations. We urge this Congress to again increase the funds available for additional inspectors and equipment in areas around the country that are experiencing the severe shortages. NTEU would also ask Congress to work to provide funding for the Customs Service in the FY2002 emergency supplemental appropriation, despite the Administration's request, which called for no appropriations for the U.S. Customs Service.

In addition to appropriations, Customs also receives funds from the COBRA account. This user fee account funds all inspectors and canine enforcement officers' overtime pay as well as approximately 1100 Customs positions across the country. This account is funded with user fees collected from air/sea passengers except from the Caribbean and Mexico, commercial vehicles, commercial vessels/barges and rail cars.

The history of collections and obligations for COBRA over the last 5 years shows a significant drawing down of reserve money available in the COBRA fund for overtime and additional positions, to the point where a significant ($40 to $60 million) shortfall could be expected in 2002. Customs anticipates collecting approximately $300 million in COBRA fees during FY2002, well below the $350 million they project in COBRA obligations during FY2002.

To help remedy this problem, the President's FY2003 budget proposes to temporarily increase two COBRA fees to raise an additional $250 million for personnel overtime and resource needs. The first involves the international air passenger fee, which would be raised from $5.00 to $11.00. The second fee increase involves the cruise vessel passenger fee, which would be raised from $1.75 to $2.00.

Unfortunately, Congress has been extremely reluctant to raise these fees in the past, so it is unlikely that this additional money will ever materialize. The Appropriations Committee must make sure that this $250 million is appropriated so that the Customs Service can continue its critically important work.

The COBRA fund will expire on September 30, 2003, unless it is reauthorized by Congress before then. However, the President's FY2003 budget does not call for the reauthorization of COBRA. COBRA must be reauthorized or Congress must appropriate additional funds to make up for the loss of the user fees.

Another issue that I would like to address is law enforcement status for Customs Inspectors and Canine Enforcement. The U.S. Customs Service Inspectors and Canine Enforcement Officers continue to be the nation's first line of defense against terrorism and the smuggling of illegal drugs and contraband at our borders and ports. Customs Service Inspectors have the authority to apprehend and detain those engaged in terrorism, drug smuggling and violations of other civil and criminal laws. For example, it was Customs Inspectors who stopped a terrorist attack planned for New Years Day 2000 by identifying and capturing a terrorist with bomb making material as he tried to enter the country at Port Angeles, Washington.

Canine Enforcement Officers and Inspectors carry weapons, and three times a year they must qualify and maintain proficiency on a firearm range. Yet, they do not have law enforcement officer status. They are being denied the benefits given to their colleagues who they have been working beside to keep our country safe. Customs employees face real dangers on a daily basis, granting them law enforcement officer status would be an appropriate and long overdue step in recognizing the tremendous contribution Customs personnel make to protecting our borders from terrorism and drugs.

There are currently bills before Congress, HR 1841 and S 1935, that would grant law enforcement status to appropriate Customs personnel.

NTEU asks all members of the committee to cosponsor these very important pieces of legislation.

The American public expects its borders to be properly defended. The government must show the public that it is serious about protecting the borders by fully funding the agencies tasked with defending the borders and laws of the United States. No organizational structure change will be successful, no matter how good it may look on paper, if the government does not provide proper funding for its border security agencies.

Thank you for the opportunity to share NTEU's thoughts on this very important issue. I look forward to working with the Committee on this and many other issues related to border security.

Mr. SOUDER. Thank you very much. As I said earlier, I hope both you and Mr. Bonner will communicate to your members the appreciation on behalf of Members of Congress, and also the American people, for all the overtime hours, for the hard work that you have been giving on the border at this critical time of our Nation's need. You had been doing it before September 11th, but everybody is aware of it now and the overtime pressure is very much appreciated. And we have met lots of your members and agents at the different borders. I asked them to testify at different field hearings, and it has been a great learning experience for us, too, to see it firsthand what you do and the challenges.

Ms. KELLEY. Thank you very much.

Mr. SOUDER. Mr. Bonner.

Mr. BONNER. Mr. Chairman and members of the subcommittee, on behalf of the National Border Patrol Council, which represents over 9,000 nonsupervisory Border Patrol employees, thank you for this opportunity to present our views on steps that can be taken to improve security and efficiency at our Nation's borders and ports of entry.

The recent events involving the INS has given new life to many proposals for organizational change, some beneficial and some detrimental. Some of these would effectively eliminate the INS, while others would absorb all or part of it into larger consolidated agencies. There are other proposals that would improve border security technologies. One of these would enhance the ability of the INS to retain its single greatest asset, experienced personnel, by authorizing an increase in the pay level of border agents and immigration inspectors.

This brings me to the most important point I wish to make this morning. The biggest problems facing the INS will not be solved by moving boxes around on an organizational chart or enhancing technology. In our view, the solution lies in two primary areas: one, holding senior managers directly accountable for their actions and/or inaction; and two, addressing the staggering attrition rate within the INS.

Accountability of high level managers must be established quickly in order to restore public confidence and employee morale. Recent calls for authority to terminate the employment of rank-and-file employees without regard to due process are misinformed. Federal managers have always had the ability to terminate the employment of any employee for misconduct or poor performance and routinely exercise this power.

Depriving employees of due process protections would do nothing to enhance accountability, but would certainly exacerbate an attrition rate that is already unacceptably high. According to statistics compiled by INS, the attrition rate for Border Patrol agents is currently about 15 percent and will probably rise to 20 percent by the end of the fiscal year.

Among immigration inspectors, the current attrition rate is 10 percent and may rise to 15 percent before the fiscal year is over. In our view, a key element of improving security at our Nation's borders is addressing the three main causes of attrition: low pay, limited lateral and promotional transfer opportunities, and lack of job satisfaction.

The National Border Patrol Council has long supported the goal of separating immigration enforcement and immigration service functions. While there will always be a need for coordination between these two functions, it seems clear that greater mission clarity for each is likely to improve the effectiveness of both.

The various consolidation proposals, on the other hand, do not have our support. While on the surface it might appear that such measures would enhance coordination and efficiency, a closer examination shows that they would have the opposite effect by creating unwieldy bureaucracies. There are over 45 Federal agencies that have some homeland security responsibility as well as thousands of State and local agencies.

In retrospect, it is obvious that none of the consolidation proposals being discussed would have prevented the terrorist attacks of September 11th. The most important step that can be taken to safeguard against future attacks is the creation of a computer data base of all suspected terrorists that can be easily accessed by all law enforcement personnel in the country. It is much more likely that a terrorist will be encountered by a law enforcement officer in the months or years that he or she is living in our country than in the moments that he or she crosses our borders. Without the tools to recognize such terrorists, however, it is doubtful that they will be detained when they are encountered.

As this subcommittee and Congress seek ways to enhance border security and find solutions for the frustrating problems at the INS, we urge you not to lose sight of the thousands of agents, inspectors and other employees who dedicate themselves to the difficult, dangerous and often thankless task of enforcing the law along our Nation's borders. As limited Federal dollars are being committed to border security initiatives, some of those funds must be directed toward keeping these experienced employees on the job.

I again thank you for the opportunity to address this subcommittee and look forward to answering any questions that you might have.

[The prepared statement of Mr. Bonner follows:]

STATEMENT OF THE

NATIONAL BORDER PATROL COUNCIL

OF THE

AMERICAN FEDERATION OF GOVERNMENT EMPLOYEES

AFL-CIO

BEFORE THE

SUBCOMMITTEE ON CRIMINAL JUSTICE, DRUG POLICY AND HUMAN RESOURCES

COMMITTEE ON GOVERNMENT REFORM

UNITED STATES HOUSE OF REPRESENTATIVES

NEW TECHNOLOGY AND ORGANIZATIONAL STEPS THAT CAN BE TAKEN TO IMPROVE SECURITY AND EFFICIENCY AT OUR NATION'S BORDERS AND PORTS OF ENTRY

PRESENTED BY

T.J. BONNER
NATIONAL PRESIDENT

APRIL 10, 2002

On behalf of the National Border Patrol Council, thank you for this opportunity to present our views on steps that can be taken to improve security and efficiency at our nation's borders and ports of entry. The National Border Patrol Council is the labor organization that represents over 9,000 non-supervisory Border Patrol employees through collective bargaining with the Immigration and Naturalization Service (I&NS), through administrative and legal proceedings, and in the halls of Congress.

The recent events involving the I&NS have given new life to many proposals for organizational change – some beneficial and some detrimental. As we speak, the House Judiciary Committee is marking up legislation that would effectively eliminate the I&NS and create two distinct immigration bureaus within the Department of Justice – one for enforcement and one for service.

Similarly, several bills have been introduced that would consolidate the Border Patrol and other federal agencies having border security responsibilities into a new Homeland Security agency. Homeland Security Director Ridge, who earlier opposed such a consolidation, now reportedly supports some variation of this concept.

In addition to the legislative proposals that would change the organizational structure of some of the agencies responsible for border security, there are some proposals that would improve border security technologies. One of these, the proposed Enhanced Border Security and Visa Entry Reform Act of 2002, would improve the accuracy and timeliness of travel document information through the use of biometric technology and provide additional resources to train and equip immigration employees. Even more importantly, it would enhance the ability of the I&NS to retain its single greatest asset – experienced personnel – by authorizing an increase in the pay level of Border Patrol Agents and Immigration Inspectors.

This brings me to the most important point I wish to make this morning. The biggest problems facing the I&NS will not be solved by moving boxes around on an organizational chart or enhancing technology. In our view, the solution lies in two primary areas: 1) holding senior managers, especially Border Patrol Chiefs and District Directors, directly accountable for their actions and/or inaction; and 2) recognizing and addressing the staggering attrition rate within the I&NS.

From our vantage point, it appears that the I&NS operates more like a series of small fiefdoms than a unified agency. Each fiefdom is controlled by a Border Patrol Chief or District Director who has very little accountability to the Commissioner or senior management of the I&NS. The Administration appears to recognize this problem and has begun to address it by proposing to eliminate one layer of bureaucracy, the Regional Directors, in its restructuring plan. Moreover, this plan would replace the current structure of 33 multi-jurisdictional districts with 9 enforcement areas and 6 service areas. But until accountability at the highest levels is restored, the implementation of national policy and even operational directives will continue to be sporadic at best.

The National Border Patrol Council is concerned by recent calls for authority to terminate the employment of rank-and-file employees without regard to due process. It is important to remember that federal managers have always had the ability to terminate the employment of any employee for misconduct or poor performance, and routinely exercise this power. Once such an action is proposed, employees currently have the right to respond to the proposal, and to appeal the manager's decision to a neutral third party if they are dissatisfied with it. This third-party review is especially important in the I&NS, which has such a poor record of sustaining removal actions that the Department of Justice has taken the unusual step of reviewing all such actions before they are initiated. Allowing the I&NS to remove employees without affording them due process would do nothing to enhance accountability, but would certainly exacerbate an attrition rate that is already unacceptably high.

According to the attached statistical chart compiled by the I&NS, the attrition rate for Border Patrol Agents was 10.2 percent in Fiscal Year 2001, has climbed to 14 percent midway through the current fiscal year, and will probably rise to 20 percent by the end of the fiscal year. Among Immigration Inspectors, the current loss rate is 10 percent and may rise to 15 percent before the fiscal year is over. No organization can be expected to effectively carry out its mission while losing so many experienced personnel. In our view, a key element of improving security at our nation's borders is addressing the three main causes of attrition:

1) Low Pay – The journeyman level for Border Patrol Agents and Immigration Inspectors is grade 9 of the General Schedule, while almost all of their counterparts in federal law enforcement are paid at grade 12 of the General Schedule, an annual difference of approximately $25,000. The proposed Enhanced Border Security and Visa Entry Reform Act of 2002 would help narrow that gap, and is an important step in the right direction. Unfortunately, this bill is only an authorization for a pay grade increase, not an appropriation. Until such time as the Appropriations Committees include funding for the increase, the attrition problem will persist and worsen.

2) Limited Transfer Opportunities – There are few lateral opportunities along the southwest border because the I&NS fills most vacancies with new-hires rather than allowing experienced agents to transfer. Additionally, the I&NS fills most of its GS-12 Criminal Investigator positions with new-hires rather than drawing from the ranks of experienced personnel. Both of these practices encourage employees to seek employment elsewhere.

3) Lack of Job Satisfaction – The current strategy of deterrence, which forces Border Patrol Agents to sit in static positions along the border, is failing in several respects. Most obviously, it does not ultimately deter anyone from entering the country illegally, as the recent census estimate of 8 million illegal aliens should amply demonstrate. The strategy is also prompting many agents to leave the Border Patrol in search of more fulfilling work.

The National Border Patrol Council has long supported the goal of separating the immigration enforcement and immigration service functions. While there will always be a need for coordination between these two functions, it seems clear that greater mission clarity for each is likely to improve the effectiveness of both. The various consolidation proposals, on the other hand, do not have our support. While on the surface it might appear that such measures would enhance coordination and efficiency, a closer examination reveals that they would have the opposite effect by creating unwieldy bureaucracies. There are over 45 federal agencies that have some homeland security responsibility, as well as thousands of State and local agencies. In retrospect, it is obvious that none of the consolidation proposals being discussed would have prevented the terrorist attacks of September 11, 2001.

The most important step that can be taken to safeguard against future attacks is the creation of a computer database of all suspected terrorists that can be easily accessed by all law enforcement personnel in the country. As it currently stands, it would take several days and numerous high-level contacts in other law enforcement agencies to search the databases of even a fraction of these thousands of agencies. It is much more likely that a terrorist will be encountered by a law enforcement officer in the months or years that he or she is living in our country than in the moments that he or she crosses our borders. Without the tools to recognize such terrorists, however, it is doubtful that they will be detained when they are encountered.

As this Subcommittee and Congress seek ways to enhance border security and find solutions for the frustrating problems at the I&NS, we urge you not to lose sight of the thousands of agents, inspectors and other employees who dedicate themselves to the difficult, dangerous and often thankless task of enforcing the law along our nation's borders. As limited federal dollars are being committed to new border security initiatives, some of those funds must be directed toward keeping these experienced employees on the job.

Increasing Loss Rates:
FY-1999 through FY-2002

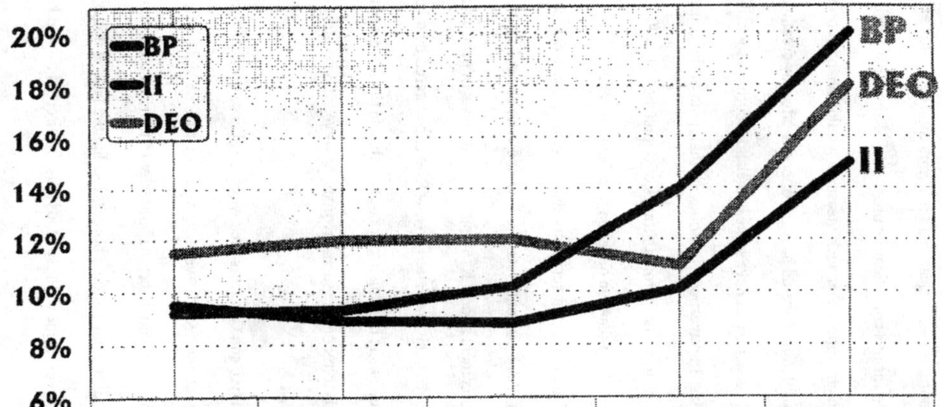

	FY-1999	FY-2000	FY-2001	FY-2002	Potential
BP	9.2%	9.3%	10.2%	14%	20%
II	9.5%	8.9%	8.8%	10.1%	15%
DEO	11.5%	12%	12%	11%	18%

Mr. SOUDER. Thank you very much for your testimony. Mr. Koch.

Mr. KOCH. Thank you, Mr. Chairman. The World Shipping Council represents the international liner shipping industry, and what the members of this industry do is they carry about two-thirds of the value of all of America's oceanborne commerce. To give you a perspective, in 2001 that was 4.8 million containers of export cargo going through our ports, 7.8 million containers of import cargo coming through our ports. Another way to think it, $1.1 billion worth of goods moving in and out of U.S. ports every single day, which goes back to the point both of you gentlemen made about the importance of trade and what is at issue here.

On September 11th we were all faced with the vulnerabilities of a free society and what America is looking at here. In the aviation context we saw what happened when four planes were hijacked, the people who were killed. From just a transportation perspective, the aviation industry was up and running—starting to be up and running 3 days after September 11th.

When you look at the ocean shipping industry, the container industry in this situation, if there were four containers which had an incident on a single day, the government's response now is not sufficiently well organized to get trade up and running in 3 days. The response, as Commissioner Bonner and the Commandant of the Coast Guard has said, would be we will close our ports. In essence, our response is we are going to blockade ourselves.

It is incumbent upon the government to develop the organizational structure and the measures necessary to put in place to make sure that we don't do that, because all that does is make our industry a bigger target for terrorists because of the economic damage that would result from such an event.

So our position is that this issue is not just about transportation. This issue is about trade. It's about the economy, the economic health of our country, jobs. And not just in our country, but with all of our trading partners as well.

After September 11th, as was stated earlier, when the Canadian border was shut down for a couple of days, or at least slowed down for a couple of days, the auto plants in Detroit almost were forced to close. It is not just auto plants in Detroit that depend on Canadian commerce, it is all of American commerce that is hooked into this intermodal international transportation network. There are many aspects of protecting this infrastructure from terrorism. There is dealing with the ships, there is dealing with the ports and the marine terminals, there is credentialing people, there is the information process about what information does the government want, when does it need it? And there is also the container itself.

Let me talk for a second about the government. I think there is pretty good understanding being developed for what the vision ought to be for international containerized shipments, and the vision is that we ought to have a secure supply chain, we ought to have an information process where the government has enough information about a container that if it has reason to want to inspect it, it can do so at the port of loading before it is put on a ship and sent to the United States. Inspecting containers in the U.S. port of discharge is the wrong time to do it, and it is the wrong place to do it.

So as we go through this, what do we need to do? We need to define and develop the rules and regulations that will create a secure supply chain. And at customs the CTPAT initiative that Bonnie Tischler talked about is an example of doing. We need to test technology development standards and implement them. We need to credential people. We need to develop an information system that allows the government to determine what containers need this inspection before loading and have those capabilities both here and abroad.

Now I recognize this is a difficult issue and our government is struggling with it. Some of the struggle is just because the issue is a hard one to deal with. But part of the struggle is also because our government is not sufficiently well organized to deal with the issue itself. I would say it has done a fine job on dealing with the issue of ships. The Coast Guard has shown leadership, both of addressing port security and vessel security in U.S. ports and at the International Maritime Organization, because responsibility is clear, they are focused on it and they are doing it.

We're doing a better job at port security, but that isn't moving quite as well along. But to undertake the steps necessary to secure the international container cargo security issue is where we are really, I think, in need of better focus. We have the Customs Service who regulates trade. They have come up with a CSI initiative and the CTPAT initiative. We have the Coast Guard who deals with ships, but also trying to deal with ports and other issues at the IMO, and now within DOT we are standing up the Transportation Security Administration where this mission has not been terribly well defined.

The U.S. Government needs focus and organizational clarity. Furthermore, we cannot persuade foreign governments to join us in doing this unless we have decided clearly within our own government what we're willing to accomplish and can speak with one coherent voice. Admiral Loy, Commandant of the Coast Guard, said 2 weeks ago when he spoke before the Port Association, we're talking about what we ought to do rather than getting on with the job of getting it done. We believe the Admiral is correct.

Some of the questions that I would submit kind of reflect this: Who is responsible for the information systems that will support enhanced security analysis? Customs, which the Senate bill addresses? Is it DOT, which the House bill addresses? What are the government's informational requirements and who is going to decide what those requirements are? Who is responsible for setting cargo security rules? Who is responsible for determining how we manage cargo security and trade if there is an incident? How are we going to manage and make sure we don't have the blockade scenario that I mentioned at the beginning of my comments?

Finally, to conclude—as our testimony does, which I ask to be put a part of the record—that four principles be kept in mind as we do all this.

First, we need to act and get legislation to facilitate this process. We need a unified strategy. One person speaking on the issue. We need clearly mandatory rules so that everybody in the supply chains know what they have to do and are held to it. We need a security regime that allows for a free and efficient flow of trade.

And finally we must reflect on the fact that if we're going to effectively extend our borders beyond U.S. jurisdiction, we need international cooperation. We need to coordinate with our trading partners, and so we will need a coherent international effort as well. Thank you, Mr. Chairman.

[The prepared statement of Mr. Koch follows:]

85-608 D-3

WORLD SHIPPING COUNCIL
PARTNERS IN AMERICA'S TRADE

Testimony of

Christopher Koch

President & CEO of the
World Shipping Council

Before the
House Government Reform Committee's
Subcommittee on Criminal Justice, Drug Policy, and Human Resources

April 10, 2002

I. Introduction

America is a free nation that generally aspires to free trade. Our international transportation and trading system reflects that relative openness and freedom, and we all benefit from it. But today we face a serious, new challenge: How best to design and implement effective maritime security measures that will successfully defend our trading and transportation system from terrorism – while preserving the efficiencies and benefits which consumers, businesses and every national economy derive from today's system.

Meeting that challenge is not a simple task. "Maritime security" covers a variety of different, distinct industries and elements, including: inland waterways, port facilities, marine terminals, non-maritime facilities located on navigable waters, bridges, cruise ships, tankers of various types, and the liner industry. My remarks today will address only the *liner shipping*[1] aspects of this agenda, which, while representing only a portion of the international maritime transportation system, are substantial enough to have produced multiple "container security" initiatives within the Executive Branch, legislative initiatives within Congress, as well as a "Sixty Minutes" story two weeks ago.

[1] Unlike bulk carriers or "tramp" ships that operate for hire on an "as needed, where needed" basis, liner vessels operate in regular, scheduled services on fixed routes. Containerized cargo is generally transported on liner vessels.

In 2001, the international liner shipping industry carried approximately 18 million TEUs (twenty-foot equivalent units) of containerized cargo in America's international trade – roughly $480 billion dollars worth of goods. That represents slightly over two-thirds of the value of all of the nation's oceanborne commerce. It represents approximately 4.8 million containers of U.S. export cargo and 7.8 million containers of import cargo.[2]

Over 800 ocean-going liner vessels, mostly containerships and roll-on/roll-off vessels, make more than 22,000 calls at ports in the United States each year. That's more than 60 vessel calls a day – providing regular scheduled services to and from virtually every country in the world. Liner shipping makes it easier and cheaper for U.S. exporters to reach world markets, and provides American businesses and consumers with inexpensive access to a wide variety of goods from around the world – strengthening our economy and enhancing our quality of life. The members of the liner shipping industry who comprise the World Shipping Council[3] carry over 90 percent of this volume. They are "Partners in America's Trade", and they recognize that this partnership requires the industry to work effectively with the government to address the new threat that terrorists might try to use or attack our transportation system.

The immediate challenges are (1) to design the security process and deploy the capabilities necessary to minimize, detect and intercept security risks as early as possible – before they are loaded aboard a ship for delivery to their destination, and (2) to have the systems and international protocols in place to ensure the efficient flow of international commerce during all possible security conditions. We must protect the system that facilitates world trade, and prevent transportation assets from becoming means of delivering destruction. We must protect the lives of people who make the international trade system operate and who work and reside in areas through which trade flows. We must protect the nation's ability to continue its trading relations in the event terrorists do attack. And, we must recognize that this terrorist threat is not going to go away, but only become more challenging to address as world trade volumes grow.

For that reason, what is at issue is not just maritime security, or even the global, intermodal transportation system, but the flow of international trade and the world's economic health.

Government officials have clearly stated their concern over the possibility that our international transportation system might be used as a conduit for terrorism. Accordingly, governments must devise and implement effective strategies to reduce and manage such risks, and carriers, shippers, ports, marine terminals, importers and third parties need to support what is necessary to achieve those objectives.

At the same time, government officials have indicated that, if terrorists were to attack this system, the government response might be to shut down trade.[4] That, however, would allow the

[2] Containers are different sizes, including 40 foot (most common), 45 foot, and 20 foot. For that reason a specific number of TEUs does not equal that number of containers, as a 40 foot container equals two TEUs.
[3] The membership of the Council is attached as Appendix A.
[4] Customs Commissioner Bonner has stated that "the shipping of sea containers would stop" if a nuclear device were detonated in a container. One can only agree with his comment that this would be "devastating", would cause "massive layoffs" in the economy, and that "we must do everything in our power to establish a means to protect the global sea container trade, and we must do it now." Speech of Commissioner Robert C. Bonner, before the Center

terrorist threat to strangle international trade. It would be extremely damaging to the American and world economy. The government must have a strategy and the capability to ensure that trade continues to flow, even if there is an incident. The alternative would create an even greater incentive for terrorists to target the transportation industry, because the consequences would be so destructive.

There is no single solution for this problem. No single government agency can solve this problem. No single government can solve this problem on its own. Every commercial party involved in the transportation of goods has a role to play. Every government has a role to play.

Shippers, consignees, carriers, ports and terminal operators all fear that in the endeavor to address these security concerns, the free and efficient flow of commerce will be impeded, and that requirements may be imposed that unnecessarily impede commerce and raise operating costs, but do little to improve security. This is an entirely legitimate concern. The answer, however, is not to delay action. What is needed is for the government to clearly identify the new security requirements, and for the industry to work cooperatively and quickly with the government to determine the best, most efficient way to meet them.

After September 11, the World Shipping Council established a Security Advisory Committee in order to consider how the liner industry could assist the government in the effort to improve security and protect the flow of commerce. On January 17, the Council issued a White Paper, which was provided to the Department of Transportation, the Customs Service and various Congressional Committees. Based on that paper and the continuing commitment of the liner industry to help the government develop effective responses to these challenges, I'd like to offer the following observations.

II. The Challenges

Designing and implementing an effective maritime security program will require cooperation, information sharing, and coordination between government and industry. At the outset, the Council recommends that the federal government's strategy and actions should be consistent with certain principles.

First, there must be a unified, coordinated federal strategy to address the issues involved not only in detecting and preventing terrorist attacks on the international cargo transportation system, but also in contingency planning and management of the consequences of such a potential event. We recognize that the Department of Transportation oversees transportation and the Customs Service oversees trade, but improving the security of intermodal, containerized cargo shipments requires a tightly integrated, common approach and clear responsibilities. It also requires government agencies to effectively share the information that they require.

Second, there should be clear, mandatory rules informing each responsible person in the transportation chain what is required of them. Voluntary programs designed to provide enhanced security levels and to expedite the transportation of low risk cargo are important and should be

---

for Strategic and International Studies, January 17, 2002, Washington, D.C.. Coast Guard officials have made similar comments.

pursued. But, effective security against terrorist threats also requires clear requirements, with clear accountabilities, which are uniformly applied and enforced.

Third, the security regime must allow for the efficient flow of trade. Efficient transportation and secure transportation are not incompatible.

Fourth, international cooperation is essential to effectively and comprehensively extend enhanced security to international supply chains. We all recognize that there are both

- legitimate concerns about unilateral U.S. actions that have international implications and about the need for international standards on many of these issues, rather than a crazy quilt of differing national laws, and
- legitimate concerns that the international community may not act with the urgency and determination that the U.S. government regards as essential.

This tension may be unavoidable, but it need not be destructive. It requires sensitivity and effective communication on all sides. It also requires action by the governments of all trading nations, because the United States cannot effectively undertake security screenings outside its jurisdiction without international cooperation.

III. <u>Various Aspects of Containerized Cargo Shipping</u>

A. <u>Ships:</u> On the issue of ship security, we fully support the various initiatives undertaken by the Coast Guard to address vessel security, both using their existing authority and in leading the initiative at the International Maritime Organization to obtain international agreement.

The Coast Guard immediately after September 11th implemented several measures to improve tracking vessels destined for U.S. ports and the crews and passengers onboard these vessels. Through its sea marshal program, implementation of safety and security zones around vessels and escorting certain types of vessels, the Coast Guard is also taking steps to prevent vessels from becoming terrorist targets or from being used by terrorists as weapons.

The Coast Guard has submitted to the International Maritime Organization (IMO) additional proposals pertaining to vessel security. Among the proposals are the designation of security officers on every vessel and in every company that owns or operates vessels; the availability of alarms or other means on a vessel to notify authorities and other ships of a terrorist hijacking; and the expedited installation on all vessels of the Automatic Identification Systems (AIS) by July 1, 2004, instead of the existing target date of 2008. AIS provides, among other things, a ship's identity, position, course and speed. The Coast Guard has also proposed to the IMO an international system for the issuance of verifiable seafarers' documents and background checks of individual seafarers.

These and other proposals were discussed at a U.S. initiated working group meeting of the IMO earlier this year. Additional IMO meetings are scheduled for later this spring and summer with a view to approving new international vessel security measures at a special IMO session in December.

It is too early to be certain which measures will be approved later this year by the IMO and thus become internationally binding requirements, but the Coast Guard's report on the IMO effort has been optimistic. As an international industry operating liner vessels with multinational crews, and under the jurisdiction of many different flag administrations, and calling ports in many different countries, the Council's member companies would prefer that, to the greatest extent possible, mandatory vessel security measures be agreed to at the international level. Clear and uniformly applied and enforced rules would create certainty and clarity for our vessels and their crews and help protect against breaches in, and of, the international supply chain.

B. Marine Terminals: The security of ports and marine terminals in this country was analyzed in the Report of the Interagency Commission on Crime and Security in U.S. Seaports (Fall 2000) and found wanting. This issue served as an impetus for the Senate legislation (S.1214) on this issue, which we have supported.

The Coast Guard, using existing statutory and regulatory authority and working with terminal owners and operators, has already implemented certain measures to increase security in and around waterfront facilities.

Earlier this year, the U.S. Coast Guard Commander for the Pacific Area issued guidelines for the individual Captains of the Port for the inspection and maintenance of adequate security measures for waterfront facilities in the Pacific Area. Developed in cooperation with industry stakeholders, these guidelines are intended for all types of maritime terminals and facilities. They cover areas such as physical property security, personnel security, passenger security, vehicle access and rail security, and are differentiated according to three risks levels. As guidelines, they do not replace or supersede existing regulations. Rather they are intended to assist the individual Captains of the Port and the operator of a facility in evaluating the security of that facility and taking corrective measures, if necessary. The guidelines are a constructive first step, but further actions are needed. For example, these guidelines do not address the issue of credentials and access controls for people at marine terminals.

The U.S. Coast Guard included in its submission to the IMO a proposal that all port facilities be required to develop and maintain security plans, and that these plans would have to be approved by the government in whose jurisdiction the facility is located according to internationally agreed standards. In addition to this proposal, the Coast Guard has also proposed that IMO agree to a mandatory requirement that every port undergo, by the government in whose jurisdiction it is located, periodic port vulnerability assessments based on internationally agreed vulnerability assessment standards. We fully support the efforts of the Coast Guard to raise enhanced terminal security at the IMO, and believe that it is essential that international port security standards be developed and implemented. The Coast Guard has also begun the process of preparing to conduct vulnerability assessments of U.S. ports, and, towards that objective, is developing a so-called "Model Port" security concept.

C. Personnel: We support legislative and Department of Transportation efforts to establish a national credentialing program, with uniform, minimum federal standards for credentialing, with a federal background check process using criminal history and national security data, and "smart card" technology for the credentialing of appropriate transportation workers. It should cover people with access to restricted marine terminal areas and to vessels, the truckers hauling the container, and other security sensitive positions. America's seaports should have systems to ensure and record that only approved people who are supposed to be there are there, and only when they are supposed to be there.

Many foreign ports have more developed security procedures than U.S. ports, and the institution of credentialing, background checks, and positive access controls at U.S. ports would be a constructive step to show the U.S. government's resolve.

We also support the Coast Guard's initiative at the IMO to establish an international credentialing and background check system for seafarers of all nations. The Coast Guard estimates that 200,000 seafarers a year come to the United States. The agency's IMO proposal is a good-faith proposal to establish an internationally accepted system that would provide enhanced security and ensure the desired freedom of movement for seafarers.

D. Containerized Cargo Security: Containerized cargo transportation presents distinct and clearly complex challenges from a security perspective (1) because of the number of different entities in different jurisdictions involved in a shipment – those involved in loading and sealing the container, documentation of the shipment, storage, trucking, railroads, inland terminals, marine terminals, and the ocean carrier, (2) because of the current lack of a clearly defined and coordinated information system to receive, analyze and act on the data determined by the government to be necessary to pre-screen containerized shipments before they are loaded aboard a ship, and (3) because of the lack of an established or coordinated global capability to inspect containers, when warranted, before they are loaded aboard ships. Accordingly, we believe that it may be helpful to look at separate, but complementary, aspects of addressing this issue.

1) Operations: We support the government establishing:

- a legal requirement that the shipper must seal a container originating in or destined for the United States upon stuffing it, and record the seal number on all shipping documents;
- the standards that such seals must meet (preferably an internationally accepted standard);
- a requirement that the party receiving the container at each interchange (e.g., trucker, railroad, ocean carrier) check and record the seal and its condition upon receipt;
- a requirement that when persons having custody must break the seal for legitimate reasons, they be responsible for affixing a new one, noting the reason, and recording the new seal number on the documentation;
- procedures for when a container is received with no seal, a broken seal, or a seal discrepancy; and
- a requirement that no loaded container be stowed aboard a vessel without an intact, conforming seal.

While the industry recognizes that seals will not by themselves solve security concerns, the Council believes the above requirements would be an appropriate step to ensure a more secure chain of custody.

2) New Equipment Technologies: Council members have offered their support for government efforts in the research, testing, development and evaluation of cost-effective new technologies that could help provide enhanced security, such as electronic seals, and container tracking and intrusion detection technology. While such technologies have not yet been sufficiently proven to have government standards and be required, carriers will continue to work with the government in testing and evaluating such possibilities. Because there are roughly 11 million existing containers serving as instruments of international commerce involving multiple national jurisdictions, it is very important that any technology standards or devices be internationally available and accepted.

3) Cargo Documentation and Government Information Requirements: Customs Commissioner Bonner and the Coast Guard Commandant, Admiral Loy, have both spoken clearly about the need for container security initiatives to "push" the nation's borders out, so that the government can acquire essential cargo shipment data in time to analyze the information and determine if further inspection of that container is needed *before* it is loaded aboard ship. The logic is clear and unarguable. The port of discharge is not the place or the time to check for terrorism.

If the vision of earlier, more effective container security is to become a reality, it requires better, earlier information about cargo shipments, and the capability to effectively inspect containers before they are loaded aboard ships. Let me turn to these issues.

The government's objective is to obtain and analyze shipment information early enough to implement more timely and effective screening. The first step is for the government to establish its information requirements – specifically, what information does it need, from whom, when, electronically delivered to what information system? This is essential, but it has not yet been done.

Each person in the shipping process has a role and information: the importer who has ordered and is purchasing the goods, the shipper who is loading the goods into the container, the carriers who are transporting the goods, and the brokers and forwarders who assist in the cargo information process. Today, the earliest information *required* by the government is the ocean carriers' cargo manifests. Most cargo manifests are electronically transmitted 48 hours in advance of arrival, but they are not required to be filed electronically and can still legally be filed in paper form at the time of vessel arrival.[5] Importers are not required by law to provide cargo information and make entry

[5] NVOCC's (which are responsible for up to 40% of the cargo in some trade lanes) are not subject to the same Customs bonding and information filing requirements as ocean carriers; they are not required to file cargo manifests for inbound shipments. They should be subject to the same information filing obligations at the same time as ocean carriers.

of the goods until five days after they have been unloaded (even more time is allowed if the goods are moving "in bond"). This is not the information process that is going to support accomplishing the government's objective. The government must determine what will.

Ocean carriers are willing to do their part. They understand that the cargo manifest is a relevant source of information, and they will submit those manifests to the Customs Service when required. It is important to recognize that this cargo information is necessarily, in the case of a sealed container, the shipper's declared cargo description. If the government determines that it needs more detailed information than is on the bill of lading and the cargo manifest, then it should obtain it from the appropriate cargo interests who possess that information.

Any government approach to addressing this issue must recognize the extensive programs currently being undertaken by the Customs Service and the information systems that they are presently operating and upgrading. It would make no sense to create a new cargo information system without, at the very minimum, addressing how it relates to the Customs Service's programs and plans, and without ensuring that what is produced is a single, logical system that meets defined, coordinated objectives. Neither shippers, carriers, nor the government would be well served by competing cargo information systems at the Department of Transportation and the Customs Service. Yet, today we face confusion, as the agencies and the Congress appear divided over who is responsible for this issue and what information system should be used to address it. New legislation is necessary to address this issue of cargo information; it is essential that such legislation provide a single, coordinated strategy and assignment of responsibilities.

Finally, we believe maritime security legislation should address export cargo, as well as import cargo. Effective attention to export cargo will demonstrate to the international community that the United States is committed to addressing security risks in a comprehensive fashion, and not just the risks involved in one direction of foreign trade.

4) <u>Container Inspection Capability</u>: There can be no argument that non-intrusive container inspection equipment[6], operated by trained personnel, is necessary, and that this is a very important government competence. The Congress has increased funding for the Customs Service for this purpose; however, a strategy for enhancing such capability in ports around the world is needed.

It is not feasible or necessary to physically inspect every container entering or leaving a port. It is necessary, however, for the government to have the capability to inspect those containers that it identifies as deserving further attention, whether that be on the basis of random selection or specific information. And the better the information

[6] The term "inspection equipment" is used generically here, but recognizes that there are different kinds of equipment (e.g., mobile, crane mounted, hand held), using different technologies (e.g., X-ray, gamma ray) with different capabilities to identify different materials (e.g., drugs, radioactivity, carbon dioxide, explosives).

about a shipment, the better the government will be able to identify which containers warrant such inspection.

Unless such inspection equipment and competence is available to government authorities, not only at U.S. ports, but also at overseas ports of loading, the government will have obvious difficulty accomplishing its objective. To be fully effective, an advanced security information system requires a way to check out a questionable container before it is loaded on a ship heading to or from a U.S. port. That's the point of advanced awareness.

Perhaps the U.S. government can convince the IMO to address this issue, although it is not apparent that any existing international organization has the authority or the intent to address this. Perhaps bilateral agreements with our trading partners can provide for this. But, it is an issue that requires immediate inter-governmental planning and execution. Inspection equipment standards should be agreed upon, and inspection capabilities and international cooperation protocols established. Delay in having this capability means that the government will have one less effective tool to intercept dangerous cargo, and to keep commerce flowing in the event of a terrorist incident.

5) Sharing Information: While there are many aspects of addressing this issue, intelligence will be a key part of securing the transportation infrastructure from terrorist's threats. Appropriate means should be developed for sharing intelligence alerts and warnings on a timely basis with designated carrier personnel.

III. Moving Forward

The Coast Guard has done a magnificent job in responding to maritime security since September 11, as has the Customs Service. Maritime security has been improved because of their efforts, and their enhanced vigilance and intelligence efforts continue. The challenge is to build on those efforts and create a more complete, unified and permanent set of security procedures and systems that can better ensure the safety of America's foreign trade.

Seven months have passed since September 11, and as Admiral Loy stated recently to the American Association of Port Authorities: "We're talking about what we ought to do rather than getting on with the job of getting it done." The Admiral is correct.

The first and most fundamental requirement of "getting it done" is for the government to clearly establish who is in charge of what. With respect to ship and port security, the Coast Guard would seem to be clearly in charge. With respect to container security issues, clear responsibility has not been assigned. The resulting confusion is not only slowing the development and implementation of an effective government response, it is confusing foreign governments, as well as carriers and shippers, all of whom are essential actors in the effort to better protect international trade.

1. *First, there must be a unified, coordinated strategy to address prevention, response and consequence management.*

The Coast Guard and the Customs Service have articulated a sound vision for the desired outcome. The vision is to have a system in place that allows the government to screen cargo containers before they are put on ships sailing for U.S. ports. Such a system may have reciprocal rights for our trading partners, such as the agreement that the Customs Service recently reached with Canada. Such a system requires analysis of the shipment information in advance of loading and possession of the capability to inspect any container the government chooses to inspect. It also requires the government to establish with clarity who has responsibility for containerized cargo security.

Today, Customs handles the "trade" aspects of these international cargo movements, and the Commissioner of Customs has actively embarked upon the development of two container security programs -- a Container Security Initiative (CSI) and the Customs Trade Partnership Against Terrorism (C-TPAT). Ocean carriers are working with the agency in these efforts. But, it is not clear which agency is responsible for cargo security or for managing the trade consequences should there be an incident. If we are ever faced with a terrorist use of a container, what agency is responsible for determining what is done to keep international trade flowing? Customs Commissioner Bonner has indicated, as have Coast Guard officials, that the U.S. government response, presumably led by the Coast Guard, could well be to close U.S. ports. What would be required to reopen them and who would make the decision to do so? What would carriers, shippers, terminal operators and ports have to do to keep American trade flowing? What would the U.S. expect foreign ports to do, and what capabilities would we expect or require of them? When and by whom will those expectations and requirements be communicated to the relevant foreign governments and to the industry? We believe that these questions remain unanswered.

There is on average over $1.3 billion worth of American exports and imports moving in and out of our ports in containers every day. That flow of goods, often moving as part of a "just in time" supply chain, keeps countless factories operating and millions of Americans employed. It does the same in the economies of all our trading partners. Its efficiency is essential to the global economy. Accordingly, it is essential that the United States government clarify which agency is responsible for the issues involving the security of international containerized cargo shipments. Let me provide a few examples of the confusion.

First, as discussed above, consider the issue of obtaining advance information for prescreening containerized shipments before they are loaded aboard vessels bound for the U.S.. Today, there is no system in place to do this. The Senate has passed legislation, which the Administration has supported, that would give the Customs Service authority to do this by expanding their existing programs – more specifically, it authorizes Customs to require carriers to file their cargo manifests earlier than today, perhaps before loading the ship. The House Transportation and Infrastructure Committee has approved legislation (H.R. 3983) that would give the DOT the authority to do this by establishing a new program to be developed within the Transportation Security Administration. While previously endorsing S.1214, the Administration has not yet expressed a preference between these approaches. In short, the government has not yet defined its information requirements – what information does it want, from whom, when, and who is to receive it? This is essential.

Second, consider the negotiations with foreign ports and governments that will be so essential to effectively implementing an extended security program. The Coast Guard has done an outstanding job at the IMO to address vessel security issue. This is due, not only to the Coast Guard's performance, but because it is clear the Coast Guard is the responsible U.S. government agency for vessel security issues. On container security and port security, who speaks for the United States? Commissioner Bonner has undertaken his Container Security Initiative in an effort to negotiate arrangements with foreign ports and governments on container security, as he has successfully done with Canada. The legislation creating the Transportation Security Administration provides TSA sufficiently sweeping authority that it may address this issue. The Coast Guard has raised container and port security issues with our trading partners at the IMO and elsewhere. Unless the Administration makes it clear who is responsible for container security issues, U.S. initiatives will be undermined by the lack of a single vision and by unavoidable confusion within foreign governments about who speaks for the United States.

Third, which agency is responsible for managing what carriers, marine terminal operators, ports, shippers, freight forwarder and brokers will have to do if our nation ever has to manage the continuation of international commerce after a terrorist incident involving a container? Logically, it should be the agency designing how to secure and manage that system in the first place. The potential economic damage from the United States imposing in effect a "blockade" on itself as a response would be so enormous[7], that it is imperative that the government address not only what is needed to detect and prevent the threat – which is critically important, but how it would keep such an attack from accomplishing its potential objective, namely crippling the economy. Clear responsibility for this issue and the planning that is required is lacking today.

The time to address and resolve these issues is now. The Department of Transportation is creating a new component of the Transportation Security Administration with a new Undersecretary for maritime and land security. The roles of TSA, the Coast Guard and the Customs Service need to be established clearly and authoritatively. The issue and its consequences are too serious to do otherwise.

. *Second, there should be clear, mandatory rules informing each responsible person in the transportation chain what is required of them.*

We believe the government should establish clear minimum requirements, with clear accountabilities assigned to the appropriate parties, and should enforce those requirements uniformly.

---

[7] See, e.g., "Global Trade: America's Achilles Heel" by Coast Guard Commandant Admiral James M. Loy and Captain Robert Ross, *Defense Horizons,* No. 7, Center for Technology and National Security, National Defense University (Feb. 2002), stating: "Given the importance of international goods and materials to the American economy, closing our borders for more than a short period is infeasible. Furthermore, with our growing reliance on just-in-time delivery of foreign goods, even slowing the flow long enough to inspect all or a statistically significant random selection of imports would be economically intolerable." (Page 1)

. *Third, the security regime must allow for the continued free and efficient flow of trade.*

The liner industry is moving over a million containers of American import and export cargo a month. Supply chain management techniques applied to this trade have provided literally billions of dollars of savings to American businesses and consumers, as well as efficiently connecting the American economy to every market in the world. Efficient transportation and secure transportation are not incompatible, and the legislative and regulatory responses should strive to preserve the benefits of an efficient, reliable transportation system, and not add unnecessary costs.

. *Fourth, international cooperation is necessary to effectively and comprehensively extend enhanced security to international supply chains.*

This is a task that will involve U.S. leadership because America is the largest trading nation in the world, and was the subject of the September 11 attacks; however, the United States government cannot extend security to foreign ports and places without other nations' engagement and agreement. Furthermore, foreign governments have legitimate concerns about the security of their transportation systems and trade flows that must be addressed. The Coast Guard has done an outstanding job of getting the IMO to deal with many of the issues involved, especially those involving ships and ships' interface with the landside terminals. That same kind of initiative needs to be taken by the United States government with our trading partners to address the remainder of the issue of establishing an effective system to protect, prescreen and, if deemed necessary, inspect containers before they are loaded onto ships. The initiative, however, cannot be only America's.

As stated earlier, effective international negotiations and agreements with our trading partners will require the U.S. government to clearly assign responsibility within itself for containerized cargo security. But the international community also needs to address the same governmental organizational ambiguity over this issue. Is this a maritime transportation issue, a multimodal transportation issue, or a customs/trade issue? The World Customs Organization has shown neither a commitment nor the authority necessary to establish a binding regulatory system designed to ensure containerized cargo security. The International Maritime Organization has discussed the issue, but has not demonstrated the ability or desire to extend its regulatory regimes to address the various requisite parties and processes on the land side of the trade. If an existing international organization does not promptly step forward with the competence and desire to address this issue, bilateral government agreements may be the most viable and expeditious way to proceed.

Any trading nation that has a substantial interest in the efficient flow of goods between it and the United States should have a keen interest in quickly establishing such close cooperative arrangements with this country to address these issues. If the U.S. government has to manage a terrorist incident involving shipping, it may permit the smooth flow of commerce only with those countries and ports that have established systems and agreements with the U.S. that provide adequate security, advance shipment information, and container inspection capabilities. As a consequence, international trading nations should view this issue as an immediate and a priority challenge. The security and continuity of international trade is at risk, and it requires international cooperation and action.

* * * * * * *

The members of the World Shipping Council transport over two-thirds of the value of all of America's oceanborne commerce and are ready and willing to help the government in its efforts against terrorism. A safe, efficient and reliable transportation system is essential to our country's prosperity and to the prosperity of all of our trading partners. I would like to thank the Committee for doing what it can to focus attention on this very important issue. The problems are complex and difficult. The people in the government and the industry want to do the right thing and address the issue effectively. As Admiral Loy said, however, we need to "get on with the job of getting it done."

Appendix A

World Shipping Council Member Lines

APL
A.P. Moller-Maersk Sealand
(including Safmarine)
Atlantic Container Line (ACL)
CP Ships
(including Canada Maritime, CAST, Lykes Lines, Contship Containerlines, TMM Lines, and ANZDL)
China Ocean Shipping Company (COSCO)
China Shipping Group
CMA-CGM Group
Compania Sud-Americana de Vapores (CSAV)
Crowley Maritime Corporation
Evergreen Marine Corporation
(including Lloyd Triestino)
Gearbulk Ltd.
Great White Fleet
Hamburg Sud
(including Columbus Line and Alianca)
Hanjin Shipping Company
Hapag-Lloyd Container Line
HUAL
Hyundai Merchant Marine Company
Italia Line
Kawasaki Kisen Kaisha Ltd. (K Line)
Malaysia International Shipping Corporation (MISC)
Mediterranean Shipping Company
Mitsui O.S.K. Lines
NYK Line
Orient Overseas Container Line, Ltd. (OOCL)
P&O Nedlloyd Limited
(including Farrell Lines)
Torm Lines
United Arab Shipping Company
Wan Hai Lines Ltd.
Wallenius Wilhelmsen Lines
Yangming Marine Transport Corporation
Zim Israel Navigation Company

Mr. SOUDER. Thank you very much. Mr. Simpson.

Mr. SIMPSON. Thank you, Mr. Chairman. I actually think I could have gotten a better seat to a Redskins game.

Mr. SOUDER. If you wanted to see them play.

Mr. SIMPSON. I'm going to echo some of what my colleagues have said. Importers and exporters are well aware, and have for years been concerned about cargo and port security, primarily because of the potential for merchandise pilferage and also to support our government's effort to keep illegal drugs out of cargo containers.

Since September 11th, we've been acutely aware of the potential for legitimate trade to be used to conceal entry into the United States of dangerous persons or weapons of mass destruction. However, we think it's important to emphasize the contribution that our international trade makes to our national security.

The United States is the strongest Nation on earth, not because we are the most populous Nation, not because we're the best endowed with natural resources or, as we like to think, because God likes us best, but because we're the richest Nation on earth. That is what gives us the power to project our policies militarily and diplomatically around the world. Anyone who talks about shutting down our trade with other countries in the interest of national security simply just doesn't understand the basis for our national security, which is our wealth. And our international trade makes a significant contribution to the economy of the United States.

So the critical thing is to balance security at the borders with maintenance of a robust international trade with other countries.

We think there are a couple of keys to doing that. One is information. It's critical that our government get information and get it in an electronic format. Whenever a piece of information required by the government has to be delivered on paper, there's a significant risk that the piece of paper in a cargo container will not be at the same place at the same time and that creates the likelihood that a container of potentially hazardous materials will come to rest at a place where it wasn't expected to be and it isn't prepared to handle it.

There is also the fact that holographic certifications or signatures are simply not as easy to authenticate as electronic signatures, so from a security standpoint alone, having information in an electronic format is critical.

A second thing, and this was referred to by Mr. Koch, is that there are 40 agencies of the Federal Government that regulate trade at the border. A simple shipment of fresh strawberries from Mexico into the United States involves information collection by seven different agencies.

Our government needs to have one agency acting as an agent on behalf of all other parts of the Federal Government as the information collector. We recommend that be the Customs Service, but we are agnostic on that. The critical thing is that there be one window through which information can be transmitted, and there has to be the potential for that information to be shared and compared among all of the agencies that collect it.

A third critical thing about the information is that we need to go to the best source. It is simply not feasible to levy more stringent requirements on carriers for the accuracy of manifest information. Carriers will never be able to authenticate the description of what's in a sealed cargo container. They can only do that if they had the opportunity to open it and examine the contents, and that's simply not feasible. So it is critical that our government look to the best source of information and not simply impose a reporting burden on the party that is nearest at hand, whether that be the importer or carrier.

A fourth point we would like to make about information is that the security response to terrorism, the commercial response, if you will, like the military response, has to be multilateral. We can't begin the security process at our borders. There are a couple of things that we think could be done to improve our security by pushing the perimeter out beyond our border.

For example, we would recommend that the trading governments of the world develop unique consignment reference identifiers for cargo so that a shipment of goods can be tracked all the way through from the exporter to the destination in the United States with a single identifying code.

A second thing we would recommend, and here I'm going to differ from everyone else who has spoken before, is that our government look a little bit differently at how we provide for security for trade coming across the border with Canada. In the interests of emphasizing a point, Mr. Chairman, I'm going to exaggerate it. I think any dollar the U.S. Government spends on personnel or security equipment on our border with Canada is a dollar that is misspent. As an amateur historian, I will tell you that one of the things I have learned is that successful generals often win their battles by selecting intelligently the place where the battle is fought. A 4,000-mile-long land border with Canada is not the place to draw a security perimeter.

So I think it is time we sit down with the government of Canada and look at the functions we perform on our border. That border has not for years performed a significant revenue function. It's not a good place to enforce our health and safety regulations. Hundreds of thousands of Canadians and Americans across the border every day. They drink the water, they eat the food, they breathe the air, they ride on public transportation, they drive on highways 5 feet away from 18-wheelers with no thought that they have entered a more risky environment. And yet we spend over $200 million a year here in the United States to enforce our health and safety regulations at the border.

So I think one of the things we need to do is to consider working with the government of Canada to create what I would call a zone of confidence in which we're satisfied that not only the health and safety standards on both sides of the border are comparable, and this is a fact that Canadian and American citizens de facto already recognize, but also that the immigration and policing functions on both sides of the border are effective and able to keep terrorists out of both the United States and Canada. Because I can tell you this: any dangerous person who can find a way into Canada will be able to cross our border. There is simply no way we can prevent that from happening.

So the critical thing is to spend the scarce resources we have in those choke points that are the entry points into North America.

The airport in Toronto, the airport at Montreal. The airports in New York and Atlanta. If we can put our resources into those choke points and pull them off the land border that we can't defend anyway, we believe we can do a much more effective job of not only facilitating trade but guaranteeing the security of all North Americans. Thank you, Mr. Chairman.

[The prepared statement of Mr. Simpson follows:]

STATEMENT OF JOHN P. SIMPSON
PRESIDENT, AMERICAN ASSOCIATION OF EXPORTERS AND IMPORTERS
BEFORE THE SUBCOMMITTEE ON
CRIMINAL JUSTICE, DRUG POLICY, AND HUMAN RESOURCES
COMMITTEE ON GOVERNMENT REFORM
U.S. HOUSE OF REPRESENTATIVES

APRIL 10, 2002

Mr. Chairman and members of the subcommittee, thank you for giving me the opportunity to appear before you today to discuss the views of the U.S. international trade community on enhancing border and port of entry security.

Our interest is plain: American companies operate in a global environment. They obtain raw materials and components from around the world for manufacturing operations here in the U.S.; they bring products from around the world for the shelves of stores not only in Manhattan and Beverly Hills but also in Fort Wayne and Muncie; they export goods made by American workers and the produce of American farms to markets around the world.

For American importers and exporters, security in global supply chains is critical. Long before cargo security became an issue that attracted the attention of the federal government and the national media it was a matter of intense interest to American exporters and importers. For years we have worked to improve container security, both to protect against merchandise pilferage and to support our government's efforts to prevent legitimate trade from being exploited to conceal smuggling of illegal drugs.

America's exporters and importers fully understand that we share the obligation borne by all other Americans to respond to the heightened security threat that our country now faces. After all, we live here too. We are working with Congress and the Administration to develop new security measures that are effective and sustainable. Our long experience with efforts to protect cargo places us in a position to give valuable advice, and to offer frank and constructive criticism about proposed security measures that will not be effective or that reflect a misunderstanding of how global commerce works.

In a commercial environment in which time really is money, and in which intermodal transportation arrangements are tightly coordinated, the rapid transmission and analysis of information is critical to the effectiveness and efficiency with which government border agencies perform their duties. That is particularly true for the U.S. Customs Service.

I speak on behalf of the members of the American Association of Exporters and Importers and their millions of employees across the country when I say that we are grateful to the Congress, and particularly to Chairman Ernest Istook's appropriations subcommittee, for the attention you have given to modernizing the automated commercial system of the Customs Service, and for the funding you provided for the current fiscal year to enable Customs to complete the new Automated Commercial Environment, or ACE, within four years.

The rapid completion of ACE has taken on new importance since September 11. We in the trade community understand that the millions of cargo containers entering and leaving the United States every year pose a significant potential security threat. A cargo container could be used to transport either dangerous persons or weapons of mass destruction into the United States. It is also possible for high-technology articles produced in the United States to be exported unlawfully to prohibited destinations. We know that we cannot allow these things to happen.

However, we know also that the flow of trade into and from the United States must not be impeded. Our national security rests fundamentally on the strength of our economy. We are the most powerful nation in the world because we are the richest nation in the world. And our robust international trade is and throughout our history has been an important contributor to our economic strength. Anyone who believes that stopping trade might ever be in the interest of national security simply misunderstands the fundamental basis of our strength.

The answer to balancing these two components of our security – border control and robust trade – lies in assuring that government agencies have essential pieces of information needed to perform risk assessment on cargo, conveyances, and people arriving in the United States. There are several keys to effective and efficient use of information for border security.

One key is assuring that information the government needs can be provided by importers, exporters, and carriers in an electronic format. Nothing is more frustrating for the trade community than to have a shipment held because a critical piece of information is missing and can only be provided on a paper form. Not only is it more costly to prepare and transmit information in a paper format but with hundreds of transactions a day it is difficult for companies to assure that in every instance a cargo container and a paper document will reach the same place at the same time.

But dependence on paper documents can also create security risks. For example, EPA rules implementing the Toxic Substances Control Act (TSCA) require importers of chemicals to certify prior to release that the chemicals are or are not subject to the TSCA. Currently, the Customs Service has made no provision to receive TSCA certificates or other EPA-required certificates in an electronic format, although EPA would very much like for that to be done. Consequently, if a paper certificate has not arrived at a port prior to arrival of a chemical shipment a Customs officer must decide either to hold that shipment of possibly toxic chemicals in a place where they were not expected to be and that is not prepared to handle them, or to release the shipment without the required certificate. It is often prudent to do the latter. Whenever a shipment of goods stops moving and is sitting largely unattended the security risks increase, and this is particularly true for a chemical shipment.

We have spoken to the Customs Service about this and are hopeful that they will address this problem soon.

A second key to effective use of information for border security is coordinating its collection and use among government agencies. There are about forty agencies of the federal government that require information at the border. Some of the information is collected on paper, as I noted earlier. But even when the information can be submitted electronically there is no single "window" through which an importer or carrier can transmit the information, there are redundant reporting requirements, there are differences in data definitions that not only add to redundancy but also prevent effective data comparisons among agencies, and there is limited capability of government agencies to communicate their findings to each other.

The International Trade Data System, which was first proposed several years ago, was intended to harmonize government trade data collection, permit data to be collected through a single channel, and enable government agencies to communicate risk analysis results with each other. This would create enormous efficiencies for the trade community and, not incidentally, improve the use of information for security purposes.

ITDS was intended to be the "front end" data collection mechanism for ACE. All data required by government agencies in connection with cross-border trade would go thought the single window of ITDS and be distributed to the agencies requiring that data. Consolidated risk assessment results would flow back through a single channel to the Customs inspector at the border.

Unfortunately, it appears that this may not happen. As we understand it, the federal agencies that need to connect to ACE have either not requested the funds, or have not been given the funds, to build the necessary links. There is apparently no place in government, either the Executive Branch or Congress, that has the authority or interest to oversee the government's information collection, and to assure that information is collected efficiently and used effectively. I understand that this subcommittee may not be in a position to deal with this problem but I believe I need to call it to your attention nonetheless in the hope that you will discuss it with your colleagues in the Congress and get the ITDS back on track.

Better coordination among government agencies does not require that they be consolidated under single management. Any private sector manager will tell you, and these days there are many who can, that corporate mergers are disruptive, and that they work only when the two organizations being merged have compatible missions and cultures.

It is understandable that one could visit a port of entry and form a first impression that there is an absence of coordination and a duplication of effort. What a new observer is likely to miss is that despite the similarity of work performed by agencies at the border their statutory missions and processes that are very different. Both the Customs Service and the Immigration Service have inspectors at the border, as do the Agriculture Department, the Food and Drug Administration, the Fish and Wildlife Service, and, increasingly, agencies concerned with transportation safety. But away from the border, Customs and INS perform quasi-judicial and administrative functions that are very different. The constituencies they serve, and the committees of Congress to which they are accountable, are different as well.

Although the importance of the Customs Service as a revenue collection agency has declined relative to the Internal Revenue Service, it is still a significant revenue generator and, more significantly, the statutes under which it operates were enacted by Congress to implement a revenue collection activity. The administrative process that accompanies the entry of merchandise into the United States is very different from that created to process the entry of persons. Functions such as tariff classification and valuation that are central to importing merchandise are simply not relevant to the entry of persons.

Consequently, while we agree that duplication and inefficiency with respect to the inspection function at the border needs to be addressed, and if fact have our own ideas for how that might be done, we believe that there would not be a beneficial outcome, indeed, might be a harmful outcome, from an arbitrary forced merger of agencies that have an obvious overlap at the border but are otherwise very different.

Mr. Chairman, let me again thank you and the members for giving me and my colleagues here today an opportunity to be heard.

Mr. SOUDER. Thank you very much. And our last witness will be brought home by a fellow Hoosier. Batting cleanup is Mr. Steve Russell, representing the trucking industry.

Mr. RUSSELL. Thank you, Mr. Chairman and Representative Cummings. My name is Steve Russell. I'm the founder and chairman and CEO of the Celadon Group, a trucking company based in Indianapolis. Celadon was established in 1985, and is the largest transporter of truckload freight between the United States, Canada and Mexico. We own and operate over 2,700 tractors and 8,000 trailers and employ about 2900 people.

Today I also appear before you as a member of the American Trucking Association or ATA. I appreciate the opportunity to speak to the subcommittee today and I want to commend you for holding these hearings at a very timely point and looking at ways of possibly further ensuring the security of operations and the efficiency of our country's land border ports of entry.

Since our inception, Celadon has handled more 1.3 million truckload crossings between the United States, Canada and Mexico, with crossing roughly 2,400 trailers per week at the Southern border and 800 per week on the Northern border. Trucking plays a critical role in trade between these countries by moving 71 percent of the value of freight between Canada and the United States and 81 percent between Mexico and the United States.

ATA and the trucking industry have been busy working with a number of government agencies, such as Customs, INS, and DOT to improve the security of motor carrier operations across our land borders. A more detailed description of these efforts is included in my written remarks that I have provided to the subcommittee. Such joint industry-government efforts will continue to work well to eradicate the potential use of legitimate commercial conveyances for moving illegal cargo and aliens across our Northern and Southern borders.

My comments will focus on two issues before the committee. One, the potential reorganization and consolidation of U.S. Government agencies operating at U.S. ports of entry and, two, the importance of working closely with Canada and Mexico to further improve the efficiency of operations and security of our borders.

ATA supports any viable realignment that can improve the operation of the U.S. border agencies to increase security and efficiency at our ports of entry. ATA's concerns are not related to the structure of organizations, however, but more in the processing of information systems that exist between the agencies. Therefore, any restructuring effort should focus on fixing the systems for processing and sharing information among the agencies.

However, members of the trade community are concerned that recent energies and efforts focused on improving Customs clearance and other clearance for cargo and people entering in and exiting the United States could be derailed. Perhaps more important, Commissioners Bonner and Ziglar from Customs and INS have asked for nongovernmental interests to provide feedback and input into the development of improved systems and technologies. ATA is actively participating in these efforts.

I would now like to talk about NAFTA and our relations with our NAFTA partners. Both Canada and Mexico, our largest and second largest trading partners respectively, play a critical role in our economic well-being. Bilateral trade with Mexico has tripled while U.S.-Canada trade has more than doubled since NAFTA began. The recently announced border security plans established with Canada and Mexico have launched a new basis for improving the operation and security of our mutual borders.

These plans compel our respective governments to improve harmonization of border operations, improve our exchange of information, and coordinate infrastructure development. ATA supports the establishment of a Northern American perimeter zone for security between Canada and the United States and believes that Mexico should be part of such deliberations as well. Such an approach would allow for protection of the external borders of North America, therefore alleviating security pressures constraining our land border operations.

Any efforts to enhance security of the movement of cargo across our common borders should not only focus on the trucking industry, but also include the movement of freight by rail and railcars or intermodal by rail.

On behalf of the ATA and its members, I urge the subcommittee, in conjunction with other House committees with oversight of border agencies, to look at the needs of our ports of entry. We must establish appropriate levels of resources, physical infrastructure, investments and technology to improve security and efficiency. Before a decision is reached to reorganize and realign border agencies into a single department, let's make sure that we have exhausted all other remedies.

Trade with Canada and Mexico is essential to our economic well-being. Therefore, it is critical that the movement of cargo across borders be done in an efficient, secure manner that relies on improved communications and coordination among our border agencies.

Mr. Chairman, ATA looks forward to continuing our cooperation with those authorities charged with securing our Nation against future terrorist threats. ATA understands the role trucking must play to ensure our national security in this newly changed landscape. Thank you, Mr. Chairman.

[The prepared statement of Mr. Russell follows:]

Statement by

Mr. Steve Russell
Chairman & Chief Executive Officer
Celadon Group, Inc.

Prepared for the

Hearing to Examine the Enhancement of Border and
Port of Entry Security And Law Enforcement

Before the Subcommittee on Criminal Justice, Drug Policy, and Human Resources of the
Government Reform Committee
U.S. House of Representatives

Wednesday, April 10, 2002

I. Introduction

Good morning Mr. Chairman and members of this Subcommittee. My name is Steve Russell, and I am Chairman and CEO of Celadon Group, Inc., a trucking company based in Indianapolis, Indiana. Celadon, established in 1985, is the largest transporter of truckload freight between the United States, Canada and Mexico. We run over 2,700 tractors and 8,000 trailers, and employ over 2,900 employees.

Today, I also appear before you as a member of the American Trucking Associations, Inc. (ATA), with offices located at 2200 Mill Road, Alexandria, Virginia 22314. ATA is the national trade association of the trucking industry. Through the affiliated state trucking associations, affiliated conferences and other organizations, ATA represents more than 30,000 trucking companies based throughout these United States. I sincerely appreciate the opportunity to speak to this Subcommittee today on behalf of my company and the ATA.

Since our inception, Celadon has handled more than 1,300,000 truckload crossings between the United States, Canada and Mexico, with roughly 2,400 weekly trailer crossings on the southern border and about 800 a week on the northern border. Celadon's Mexican trucking operation, Jaguar, provides Celadon customers with international door to door service within Mexico and brings local expertise to transportation between points in Mexico and the U.S. border. In 1998, Celadon acquired Gerth Transport Ltd. in Canada, completing Celadon's lane strength from Mexico to Canada.

Mr. Chairman, for the purposes of this hearing, I will touch on various efforts our industry has been leading and participating in to ensure the security of the trucking industry, and in specific those with cross-border trucking operations, including:

- Establishing an industry-wide Anti-Terrorism Action Plan (ATAP) in partnership with various other trucking related associations and interest groups to enhance the security of motor carrier operations throughout North America;

- Working with U.S. Customs to develop the trucking industry's participation in the Customs Trade Partnership Against Terrorism (TPAT) to ensure the security of the international supply chain;

- Contributing to U.S. Customs' Trade Support Network to develop a state of the art Customs clearance system, the Automated Commercial Environment (ACE), and its front end system, the International Trade Data System (ITDS);

- Participating in the Department of Justice Data Management Improvement Act Task Force to assist the Immigration and Naturalization Service (INS) establish an entry and exit control system; and

- Advising the U.S. Department of Transportation (DOT) in its efforts to ensure the security of multi-modal container movements as they arrive and depart our country.

I will also make some brief comments regarding:

- The potential reorganization and consolidation of U.S. government agencies operating at U.S. ports of entry and possible implications of undertaking such an effort; and

- The importance of working closely with Canada and Mexico to improve coordination, including the potential establishment of a North American Perimeter Security Zone.

II. ATA's Involvement in Transportation Security and Related Issues

First however, it is important to state that ATA and its members have long been actively involved in providing safe and secure transportation of goods on behalf of our customers and their consumers. Since 1982, ATA has maintained a Council of members dedicated to advancing security and loss prevention issues. The name of this organization has undergone numerous changes since its inception, and today is known as the Safety & Loss Prevention Management Council (Safety Council). The Safety Council has two committees, the Security Committee and the Claims and Loss Prevention Committee, that have addressed many trucking security issues, including driver and vehicle security, cargo security, and facility security. The committees consist of security directors, many of whom are former law enforcement personnel, from a broad array of America's leading motor carriers. The committees publish guidelines and educational materials to assist motor carriers enhance the security of their operations.

Although the Safety Council has worked primarily on issues related to cargo theft, having such a strong ongoing security effort has served us well in the aftermath of September 11. Since the terrorist attacks, motor carriers throughout the trucking industry have taken a number of measures to increase the security of their operations. Some motor carriers have re-evaluated their overall security procedures for pick-up and delivery, for their service locations, terminals and loading-dock facilities, for dispatch operations to vehicles in cities and on the road. In addition to requesting their personnel to be extremely alert and to report any suspicious activity to law enforcement personnel, many motor carriers have initiated new background checks through systems available to motor carriers, and emphasized to all trucking company employees, not only drivers, to stay alert and remain aware of their surroundings at all times, especially when transporting certain types of cargo.

Mr. Chairman, in the wake of the September 11 attacks, the U.S. trucking industry has continued to work hard to support America's goal of keeping our country and our economy moving forward. As members of this Subcommittee know, motor carriers are a critical component of the United States' economic strength, with 9 billion tons of freight transported by inter-city and local trucks, representing 68% of the total domestic tonnage shipped. The trucking industry generates revenues of $606 billion annually, equaling almost 5% of our GDP, and a figure that represents nearly 87% of all revenues generated by our nation's freight transportation industry[1].

But furthermore, trucking plays a critical link among the economies of the United States, Canada and Mexico, moving over 71 percent of the value of freight between the United States and Canada, and about 81 percent of the value of U.S.-Mexico freight[2]. Certainly, the increasing trade volumes that have been generated among the three North American Free Trade Agreement (NAFTA) partners have not only been good for the economic well being of our countries, but have also increased business revenues for trucking companies that provide cross-border trucking services.

As in all other sectors of our country's economy, the attacks of September 11 have heightened security concerns, including for motor carriers operating across our borders with Canada and Mexico. As the members of this Subcommittee are probably aware, on September 11, ports of entry at our international land borders were put on Level 1 Alert, resulting in extreme crossing delays, and severely hampering delivery of parts and equipment for just-in-time deliveries at manufacturing operations. Although the severe delays lasted only a few days thanks to the increased deployment of personnel by U.S. Customs and the assistance of the national guard, crossing times are still not at levels as those prior to the attacks on our nation.

I want to commend you, Mr. Chairman, for holding this hearing today to look at possible ways of further ensuring the security of operations at our country's ports of entry. It is critical that, as we look to further bolster the security of cross-border operations, we keep in mind the vital role that international trade plays in our economy. As we move forward in developing policies to implement heightened security measures at our ports of entry, we must also look at ways to improve the efficiency with which legitimate trade moves in and out of our country.

Trucking Industry's Anti-Terrorism Action Plan

In producing the Anti-Terrorism Action Plan (ATAP), trucking industry representatives are developing a blueprint for establishing a joint industry-government effort to mitigate the possibility of a truck conveyance from transporting or being used as a weapon of mass destruction. The trucking industry has developed a plan that closely follows the guidelines established by the Office of Homeland Security. ATA recognizes that this proposed plan represents only one segment of our nation's supply chain, and that a broader effort to include manufacturers, retailers, brokers and others will be necessary to further improve the security of our nation's infrastructure and economic well being.

---

[1] *Freight Transportation Forecast...2011*, Prepared DRI-WEFA for TT Press (ATA), 2002
[2] Bureau of Transportation Statistics, U.S. Department of Transportation.

ATA expects to make an announcement for final publication of the ATAP within the next few weeks. I want to assure Members of this Subcommittee that the trucking industry is ready to work closely with government agencies and other members of industry in protecting our Nation from future attacks.

U.S. Customs Programs and Systems

Land Border Carrier Initiative Program and Trade Partnership Against Terrorism

It is important to note that high-security environments are not new for motor carriers that participate in cross-border operations with Canada and/or Mexico. For instance, the trucking industry, in a joint effort with U.S. Customs, developed in 1995 the Land Border Carrier Initiative Program (LBCIP). This program was designed to counter the smuggling of illegal cargo, including narcotics and aliens, via commercial land carriers and land conveyances. The LBCIP was designed for carriers to provide background information on drivers and trucking companies moving cargo across the U.S.-Mexico border. Although the initial intention was to implement the LBCIP only on the U.S. southern border, when U.S. Customs published its final rule on the program in 1998, it left open the possibility of its implementation on both land borders.

Today, U.S. Customs is considering the use of the LBCIP as a platform from which to include motor carriers with cross-border operations under the Customs' Trade Partnership Against Terrorism (TPAT) umbrella. The overall goal of Customs' TPAT is to ensure the security of the entire international supply chain: from overseas manufacturing operations, to air, sea and land transportation providers, to entities such as brokers and forwarders involved in the processing of cargo entering our country.

Joint industry-government efforts, such as the TPAT, the LBCIP and others, like the Business Anti-Smuggling Coalition (BASC), an industry driven voluntary effort to increase security in the movement of international trade, have allowed the trade community and law enforcement agencies to share information and improve security for the transportation of international cargo. Such joint efforts will continue to work well into the future to eradicate the flow of illegal and/or dangerous cargo or aliens from entering the United States in commercial conveyances and increase the security of our operations as we move cargo across our northern and southern borders.

Development of Automated Commercial Environment and International Trade Data System

The trucking industry also asks the Subcommittee to look at technologies under development that can facilitate enforcement efforts while at the same time expedite the movement of cargo across our borders. One such system being designed presently by U.S. Customs is the Automated Commercial Environment, or "ACE".

In 1993, along with legislation implementing the NAFTA, Congress passed the Customs Modernization Act, or "Mod Act", establishing a new operating environment for U.S. Customs and the international trade community. Concepts such as "informed compliance," "shared responsibility" and "reasonable care" imposed greater obligations on U.S. Customs to provide improved information concerning the responsibilities and rights of the trade community. At the same time, the legislation mandated U.S. Customs to develop a new automated customs processing system, to replace the antiquated and overburdened Automated Customs System (ACS). Nearly ten years after the passage of the Mod Act, ACE is still in its nascent stage, but it is finally under significant development, and its full deployment is expected within the next three to four years. The present head of U.S. Customs, Commissioner Robert Bonner, has recognized the importance of developing such a system to give Customs greater tools to improve its information collection and improve the efficiency with which it processes millions of transactions every year.

As part of its development of ACE, U.S. Customs is also developing the International Trade Data System (ITDS) to operate as its front-end data capturing system. The ITDS concept is simple: Traders and carriers submit commercially based, standard electronic data records through a single federal gateway for the import or export of goods. As a single information gateway, ITDS distributes these records to the affected federal trade agencies, such as U.S. Customs, INS, FDA or DOT, for their selectivity and risk assessment. In standardizing the process, ITDS reduces the confusion and complexity of international trade, and speeds the processing of goods, equipment and crews across our borders. ITDS also benefits the government by providing more current and accurate information for revenue, public health, statistical analyses, and safety and security activities, as well as significantly reducing data processing development and maintenance costs.

Mr. Chairman, it is important that Congress continues to provide adequate funding for the full development and implementation of the ACE system. In order to defend our Nation from potential future terrorist attacks, and at the same time process the legitimate commercial goods so important to our nation's economy, we must provide our border enforcement agencies the necessary tools and resources to fulfill their duties and responsibilities.

DOJ's Data Management Improvement Act Task Force

In 1996, Congress passed the Illegal Immigration Reform and Immigrant Responsibility Act, which included the creation of an entry exit control system at land, sea and airports. Section 110 required the INS to develop an automated entry and exit control system that would collect a record of every alien arriving and departing the United States and match the record of departure with the record of the alien's arrival in the United States. This would be a requirement for all non-U.S. citizens, including U.S. permanent residents.

With over 400 million crossings of individuals, and over 11 million truck crossings at our northern and southern land borders a year, Section 110 would have caused extreme delays and back ups at ports of entry, causing further delays for truckers who operate in an increasingly demanding just-in-time delivery environment. Section 110 would have negatively impacted the U.S. economy by disrupting the operations of U.S. trucking firms with cross-border operations.

After a series of negotiations to amend Section 110, "The Immigration and Naturalization Service Data Management Improvement Act of 2000" was passed to improve the management of data on entries and exits collected under current law, without imposing additional entry-exit controls. The bill had four basic goals for the INS:

1. To continue to collect the data it was already collecting;
2. To set up databases to integrate the data it collects at airports, land border ports of entry, and seaports;

3. To record who's coming in and who's going out, and match those records to the extent possible; and

4. To improve the operations of these systems over time with the latest technology available.

The legislation also established a "task force" with private sector and state and local government participation. The task force is now fully operational and has conducted a series of meetings to move forward the development of an entry and exit control system. The task force is evaluating how the Attorney General can efficiently and effectively carry out the amended Section 110 and how the United States can improve the flow of traffic at airports, seaports, and land border ports of entry. In addition, the Attorney General is encouraged to consult with affected foreign governments, such as Mexico and Canada, to establish reciprocal, mutually beneficial mechanisms to improve border management cooperation.

U.S. Department of Transportation Initiatives

NAFTA Trucking Provisions

Mr. Chairman, ATA supports the implementation of NAFTA's trucking provisions in order to improve the efficiency with which cross-border operations take place between the U.S. and Mexico. ATA is also a strong advocate for ensuring that all carriers operating in the U.S. – Canadian, Mexican or U.S. carriers – meet all U.S. safety and environmental standards, as well as all financial operational responsibilities. To this end, DOT recently published in the *Federal Register* a number of regulations regarding the application process and operating requirements for Mexican motor carriers who want to obtain operating authority to operate in the United States.

The issuing of these regulations by DOT is important because they underscore a fundamental principle for operating in the United States: NAFTA's trucking provisions do not represent an open door policy for all Mexican carriers to operate into the U.S. A Mexican carrier that wants to operate in the U.S. must first apply ***and*** receive operating authority to do so, to include getting the necessary insurance coverage. Each Mexican motor carrier will have to apply through a thorough application process and be approved by the U.S. Department of Transportation. Mexican motor carriers will have to demonstrate that they understand and are able to meet all U.S. standards and requirements applicable to all U.S. motor carriers. If approved by DOT, they will get a conditional operating authority, which will become permanent once they have successfully undergone a comprehensive safety compliance review within an 18-month period.

Furthermore, implementing NAFTA's trucking provisions would enhance the security of cr border trucking operations by simplifying the movement of trailers across our common borders. Ir report to Congress issued in 1997 by the White House on U.S.-Mexico anti-drug cooperation, the I Customs Service wrote:

> ***The high congestion of truck traffic entering the United States is, in part, a result of restrictions imposed by both the United States and Mexico on crossborder motor carrier operation... over 50% of commercial trucks enter the United States empty, contributing to border congestion and increasing the inspection burden for border agencies.***

Therefore, NAFTA's trucking provisions allow for carriers throughout North America, such as Celadon, to improve our ability to make cross-border trucking more efficient, effective, safer, and more secure.

DOT Security Direct Action Groups

As part of its efforts to work with federal agencies to harden potential truck industry targets against terrorists, ATA has participated actively in DOT's efforts to protect America's transportation infrastructure. The DOT established Direct Action Groups (DAGs) to study, in conjunction with industry, how to strengthen potential security weaknesses in our transportation system. Industry representatives, including ATA, have been participating in the DAGs providing advice and serving as communication links with transportation providers. The Credentialing DAG is focused on criminal background checks and identification cards for all transportation workers at all federal, state and local facilities.

On January 22, the DOT National Infrastructure Security Committee's (NISC) Credentialing Direct Action Group (CDAG), a DOT-wide, multi-modal working group, briefed industry on its concept for a national transportation worker I.D. card (TWIC). ATA is encouraged by the initial work of the CDAG and agrees that a TWIC could be tailored to fulfill the security needs of the various modes of the transportation chain and reduce the need for redundant criminal history record checks and credentials. With a properly designed TWIC, only one card would be necessary to gain access to secure areas requiring background checks for criminal history records.

A properly designed TWIC will eliminate the need to bear the costs of unnecessary, duplicative criminal history record checks. A properly designed TWIC will also reduce the burden on the FBI to conduct redundant criminal history record checks. The card would have the capacity to provide additional features, as dictated by the particular mode in which the transportation worker is employed.

Now Mr. Chairman, I would like to offer ATA's position on two key areas of importance to the operation of cross-border truck movements on our borders with Canada and Mexico.

Potential Reorganization of Border Agencies

Recently, there have been discussions in Washington policy circles about merging the federal agencies that play a primary role in guarding our nation's ports of entry. From Capitol Hill to the White House, various potential plans are circulating for bringing together such agencies as the INS, Customs, Coast Guard, and Border Patrol under a single department. The recent well-publicized missteps regarding visas issued to the terrorists of September 11 highlight the deep-seated procedural problems that point out the need for substantial reform.

Mr. Chairman, ATA supports exploring any viable realignment strategy that would improve the operation of U.S. border agencies to increase security and efficiency at our ports of entry. ATA believes that the problem lies in the processing systems of the border agencies and that any restructuring effort should focus on fixing the systems and mechanisms for processing and sharing information among the agencies.

If such processing deficiencies could be fixed by reorganizing our border enforcement agencies into a single agency, our industry would very likely support such a proposal. However, members of the trade community are concerned that recent energies and efforts focused on improving clearance systems for cargo and people entering and exiting the U.S., such as the development of ACE/ITDS by U.S. Customs and the DMIA task force work with INS, could be derailed. Instead of focusing on procedures and systems, work might concentrate on merging organizational cultures, and other structural issues that could easily distract agency officials from undertaking more fundamental changes: improving information sharing, and integrating information systems and databases to expedite enforcement activities more effectively and efficiently.

Again, Congress and President Bush should fully explore all potential alternatives to achieve the best possible results. But we must recognize that at issue are the processing systems and mechanisms within the agencies, for which the creation of a new government super enforcement agency may not necessarily be the best solution. The present leaders of Customs and INS, Commissioners Bonner and Ziglar respectively, are capable managers that have set out to work within their agencies to improve their operating systems and establish accountability for failures. Perhaps more important, both commissioners have asked for input from non-governmental organizations in the development of systems in their respective agencies. For instance, U.S. Customs has established the Trade Support Network to assist in the development of ACE, while the Data Manage Improvement Act Task Force is providing input to INS in the development of an entry/exit system.

Working with our Partners in Canada and Mexico

Both Canada and Mexico, our largest and second largest trading partners respectively, play a critical role in our economic well being. Consider how much the trade relationship among the three NAFTA partners has grown: from 1993 to 2001, trade in goods and services between the U.S. and Mexico increased from $81 billion to $233 billion, while U.S.-Canada trade grew from $211 billion to $381 billion[3]. As I mentioned in the introduction of this document, it is essential that we highlight the critical link that motor carriers play in moving the increasing trade flows within North America. In 1994, trucks moved $74 billion worth of U.S.-Mexico goods, while in 2000, we transported over $171 billion. With Canada, in 1994 trucks moved $168 billion worth of goods, and $258 billion in 2000[4].

Recognizing the importance of our relations with Canada and Mexico, President George W. Bush has worked with President Fox of Mexico and Prime Minister Chretien of Canada to establish cooperation agreements with our two largest commercial partners. The recently announced 30 point border security plan established with Canada, and the 22 point plan agreed to with Mexico last month have launched a new basis for improving the operation and security of our mutual borders. Both of these plans recognize our commercial interdependence and symbolize the viability of our economic, social, political and security relationships.

Shortly after September 11, the U.S. Ambassador to Canada, Paul Cellucci, proposed the vision of setting up a North American Perimeter Security Zone between Canada and the United States. Although it is well recognized that there are inherent differences among U.S.-Canada policies, ATA encourages the development of such a security partnership, and, in fact, believes Mexico should be part of the deliberations to make such an effort truly North American in nature. Such an approach would create a perimeter clearance zone, allowing for protection of the

---

[3] U.S. Top Trading Partners;International Trade Administration, U.S. Department of Commerce
[4] Bureau of Transportation Statistics; U.S. Department of Transportation. Includes exports and imports for all surface modes, by value.

external borders of North America, therefore alleviating security pressures constraining our land-border commercial operations.

These plans compel our respective governments to improve harmonization of border operations and infrastructure development to establish technology and mechanisms to facilitate and expedite the gathering, sharing, and exchange of information and data to clear cargo and people moving through our land borders efficiently and securely.

III. Conclusion

On behalf of ATA and its members, I urge the Subcommittee to continue to look at ways in which security and efficiency can continue to be enhanced at our ports of entry. We encourage you to work in conjunction with other House Committees and Subcommittees with oversight of border agencies, to analyze the appropriate levels of resources, infrastructure and investments in technology that these agencies need. The development of technologies, such as those being envisioned under ACE and ITDS, in addition to non-intrusive inspection systems such as Gamma and X-ray machines that can scan entire trailers in minutes, should also be encouraged to ensure the security of our Nation and to facilitate the processing of legitimate trade.

We must continue to find solutions that improve the processing of the legitimate flows of people and cargo, while simultaneously improving our security through stronger relationships between the trade community and law enforcement agencies at our borders. If it is necessary to reorganize and realign those agencies that operate at the border into a single department in order to improve their effectiveness, let's make sure that we have exhausted all other alternatives before undertaking such a major endeavor. Again, at present there are efforts at the INS and Customs to streamline and modernize the systems for clearing cargo and people entering our country. Our industry's concern is that all the resources, time, and efforts already invested in redesigning such systems could possibly go to waste if they were to come to an end during a restructuring process.

In addition, as a Nation, we need to look for ways to improve coordination with our counterparts in Canada and Mexico, to enhance harmonization of our border infrastructure, and integrate our technologies and information systems.

Mr. Chairman, as the Subcommittee can see from this testimony, ATA and the trucking industry have been busy at work with numerous government agencies to enhance the security of trucking operations throughout North America. ATA members understand they are entrusted with the secure transportation of goods that keeps America moving forward. Law enforcement has frequently been a strong ally in ATA's longstanding efforts to ensure the security of cargo on America's highways and across our international borders. We look forward to continuing our cooperation with those authorities charged with securing our Nation against future terrorist threats. ATA understands the role trucking must play to ensure our national security in this newly changed landscape.

Mr. SOUDER. Thank you very much. One of the frustrations that you have when you plunge in an area, it reminds me of when I was in high school, my dad found this plaque that he thought was hilarious and he brought it home from vacation to the band director. And we all had to sit every time we had band and look at this plaque, and he thought it was hilarious. None of us got it. It said, "Why can't all life's problems come when we are young and know all the answers?" .

The older you get, the more you realize the truth of that statement. And the more you plunge into this, the more difficult it is. And let me—we will go at least two rounds here because I have quite a few questions and will submit.

But let me first start with Ms. Kelley and Mr. Bonner. We are looking in our report that I chaired with Parliamentarian Susan Wayland of Windsor the U.S.-Canada parliamentary subgroup on transborder issues. And Windsor-Detroit presents a huge problem area of how to locate enough facilities to keep the traffic moving. And one of the discussions, also there are concerns on the Canadian side about moving over the bridge, if there are safety concerns. And so they've been, as well as other locations, pushing for facilities on the Canadian side.

What is the position on either of your unions of having any of your personnel based in—across the border and what concerns do you have about that?

Ms. KELLEY. NTEU currently represents some Customs employees who do in fact work in the preclearance areas in Canada, and so they are there, and there are processes for how it's determined which employees will go there, for how long, and other safety concerns. There is an issue over there concerning their inability to carry weapons, which in the United States, of course, Customs inspectors are armed.

But on the bigger issue of whether that should be expanded to more ports, I really cannot give a NTEU position at this time primarily because we have had, other than your statement, no briefings from Customs on anything that has even been considered in this area. It is something that I would like to seriously consider and needs to be addressed one way or the other as we hear about all the problems that the Customs as well as trade and the government are facing. But without a lot more information, at this point I would have to delay my response, but I would look forward to the opportunity for the briefing and for more information actually about your meetings because I just don't have that information.

Mr. SOUDER. Particularly as we look at even more complex questions of if we would move to focus at the origin of seaport traffic, as opposed to looking at it here, these become big questions on the involvement of U.S. personnel and what restrictions we have and the safety and the clearances. Even at the Ottawa airport, which has been traditional, there are concerns about safety, about the ability of both, as I understand, both INS and Customs, even if you spot somebody who is a potential terrorist, and they get any idea that we are spotting them, they can move and it may take multiple levels of the Canadian Government, which is the most cooperative of governments and the most similar to our system, to respond, and we quite frankly usually lose them.

RCMP has been cooperative. Other agencies have been less so, I think it would be fair to say. Mr. Bonner.

Mr. BONNER. As Ms. Kelley says, the biggest concern we have is the inability of our officers to be armed in Canada, and that terrorists and other criminals are going to be armed. So in order to defend ourselves and to defend the public around us, I think that is critical. So there has to be some way to overcome that if we are going to have our officers operating in foreign countries.

Mr. SOUDER. Would pursuit be a question as well?

Mr. BONNER. Depending on how it's structured. I mean, if they're going deeper into the foreign country, then obviously it is their problem and not a problem of ours. If we have the ability to shut down the lanes at the ports of entry, I don't think it would be a problem coming into the United States.

Mr. SOUDER. Because we have had this hot pursuit question at Port Angeles where we caught the millennium bomber. They went beyond their bounds and took it into their own hands or we would have lost the millennium bomber as well. These are tough questions at the borders that your agents are dealing with: Doing what they sense is the right thing to do versus doing what they are told they are supposed to do.

One other question I wanted to ask both of you on upgrading the data base and automated systems: Do you believe that there is sufficient progress being made and could you give us any insights into the ACE system?

Ms. KELLEY. The problem with the ACE system, all along in the very beginning the funding was not provided to get it off to a jump start. The information that I have to date on the ACE system is, as Bonnie Tischler testified, it is still progressing. It is still a funding issue, but it is one that I believe will address most, if not all, of the issues that we consistently hear identified that need to be addressed in the trade area.

I think everyone wishes it could happen in 6 months, not in 4 or 5 years. That has been the interest from the very beginning because of the stretch and the stress that is being put on the ACS system, as well as the employees that are trying to operate in that environment. It would be a big help to them being able to more effectively doing their jobs. If there was a way to speed up the funding, assuming that this data base work and all the technology work could be done, and I think it could be done faster than 4 years if the funding were provided, that would be, I think, a help not just to Customs, but to everyone who is depending on it.

Mr. SOUDER. Do you have any comments on that, Mr. Bonner?

Mr. BONNER. No, I believe that——

Mr. SOUDER. We will give you some written questions on the INS clearance processes on the visas and see if you have any—or either of you can in the additional days here for testimony get any input from field agents that they may have about some concerns about where we have look at how to make the systems better. We are not looking how to set us back but how to make them more effective. Mr. Cummings.

Mr. CUMMINGS. Thank you all for your testimony. It has been very interesting. Mr. Bonner, what is the rationale for limiting the lateral transfer opportunities for personnel along the southwest border?

Mr. BONNER. Cost savings. If they hire new people and put them in the desirable locations, they don't have to pay the transfer costs of experienced personnel. But in the end, you end up paying more because your experienced personnel leave because they can't get out of their initial duty assignment.

Mr. CUMMINGS. Chairman Souder has mentioned offering incentives for language proficiency, as in Spanish, for example. Do you have a view on this?

Mr. BONNER. Actually, that has been authorized since the passage of the Federal Law Enforcement Pay Reform Act of 1990 or 1991. But it's never been paid. It's discretionary with the agency. They have the ability to pay a 5 percent foreign language bonus, but have chosen never to pay a penny to their employees.

Mr. SOUDER. We also heard at the Quebec border that a number of—I can't remember if it was INS or Customs person actually grew up in a French-speaking household and couldn't meet the standards even though his first language was French, because it's State Department criteria for very formal French. And that one of the things when we are looking at languages is because we focus so much on Spanish, even in the Quebec border, you would think we would have somebody who could be certified to speak French.

So one of the things, in addition to hearing here that they aren't giving the bonuses, is is the standard expectation so high the agencies don't go after it, in addition to they don't believe they are going to get the money? This has become huge in the question of Arabic, Farsi, other languages where we basically get on a phone and you try to find the service that can interpret what that package says in a car or a truck, which probably is not written in English.

Ms. KELLEY. If I could add in the Customs Service, NTEU has been successful in negotiating with Customs over establishing some criteria for payments of the foreign language awards for recognition of that. And you are right, it is under the State Department criteria, but we have been successful in setting up joint criteria, and there are persons in the Customs Service receiving these awards, perhaps not to the extent we would like to see it paid, but Customs is making those payments to employees today.

Mr. CUMMINGS. There was another part to my question I did not finish, so we have been answering a partial question. I was just wondering, with that incentive in mind, do you all see that as a way of retaining people and attracting folk? I know the problems that you just stated.

Ms. KELLEY. In my experience, it is not anything that necessarily serves as a huge retention factor. It's not a high percentage of salary or anything that really, you know, would be a retention incentive, for example. And for the most part, we see them existing on the southwest border mostly in the language of Spanish. I really haven't seen statistics for the different languages, and in light of this conversation, I am going to get more information about what languages employees do have and where they are receiving this. I will also check on their belief concerning its retention value. I think it probably needs to be a higher percentage available to them and more actual funds available in order for that to really be a factor. But I'll check on that and get back to you, Mr. Cummings.

Mr. CUMMINGS. I appreciate that. I was getting ready to ask Mr. Bonner did he know what percentage of the immigration inspectors on the southwest border speak Spanish. Do you have any idea?

Mr. BONNER. All Border Patrol agents are required to be somewhat fluent in Spanish. They undergo a number of weeks of foreign language training and are tested twice during their probationary period, and if they are not proficient enough, their employment is terminated. Similarly, immigration inspectors all receive foreign language training. So the percentage along the Southern border is 99 percent who speak Spanish very well. And obviously on the Northern border, you have folks who are fluent in French.

I would say that it would be a help if we could get this mandatory to have this 5 percent bonus in retaining people. But bear in mind that the differential between the base pay of these employees, both the Border Patrol agents, immigration inspectors, and Customs inspectors is far behind that of most other Federal law enforcement agents.

The journeyman level is GS–9 compared to GS–12 for most other agencies. When you factor in the differences between both base pay and the overtime pay, which for the higher-graded agents is obviously paid at a higher level, you are looking in the neighborhood of about $25,000 per year.

So it is no surprise that a lot of those agents are looking for better-paying jobs. The fact that so many Border Patrol agents are going over to the Air Marshal Program now is only indicative of this dissatisfaction with the job which has been simmering under the surface for all of these years. They have just been waiting for someone else to open up jobs. Now that they have, fully half of the Border Patrol agents have applied for those jobs and——

Mr. CUMMINGS. Half?

Mr. BONNER. Fully half. The INS estimates that the attrition rate will hit 20 percent by the end of the year. We believe that it will be closer to 25 percent. That is one out of every four agents will have left, primarily for the Air Marshal Service.

Mr. CUMMINGS. So what are you doing to replace them? I mean, do you have an aggressive program?

Mr. BONNER. Yes. It has an aggressive hiring program, but their biggest problem is hanging on to the people that they have. And unless that is addressed, we can hire from now until the end of the beginning of the next millennium, and we are still going to be having this problem.

Mr. CUMMINGS. What does a GS–9 make?

Mr. BONNER. A GS–9 makes in the neighborhood of mid-30's.

Mr. CUMMINGS. Uh-huh. Just one other question.

Do you know, Mr. Bonner, whether within the INS leadership there is any kind of support for a single terrorist data base?

Mr. BONNER. I am unaware. I don't know.

Mr. CUMMINGS. All right. Does anybody else?

All right, Mr. Chairman.

Mr. SOUDER. Mr. Simpson, as to your Canada proposal, do you have a similar feeling about Mexico?

Mr. SIMPSON. I think, Mr. Chairman, the logical extension of my argument is that at some point we would have to consider the same sort of arrangement with Mexico, because that border is equally difficult to patrol. And I think the Government of Mexico, frankly, being aware that the idea of a zone of confidence between the United States and Canada has been considered, is interested in not being left out.

What I have learned is that they realize that the potential for the United States and Canada to enter into that sort of an arrangement is more advanced. Mexico understands that arrangement will come first between the United States and Canada. They just want to be on the same track, even if they are farther behind on the track. They would like to be sure that they are on the same track.

Mr. SOUDER. I think it is—a couple of things are relatively safe to say, because one is—is that most of us are aware that there are differences in the north and south border, but politically to separate the two is almost impossible. It has been a stumbling block for years, long before September 11th. And with the shifting population mixes in the United States, it is even more politically difficult, without enunciating further; that regardless whether it is based on merit or perceived discrimination, that—a second thing is that we are trying to move with the Canadians toward more commonality, but to some degree this threatens Canadian self-identity as much as it does American self-identity. In other words, they are proud of their visa differences and their immigration differences.

They have made some movement, but when we were up in Ottawa and met with the Attorney General and the parliamentarians, they have made some movement, but they aren't really interested in, quote, becoming like the United States and our more restrictive immigration policies, which is a huge stumbling block.

Furthermore, in spite of efforts, and we have made some progress, they have substantially different opinions on narcotics, particularly on BC Bud, which is going on the streets of Fort Wayne and New York for more than cocaine right now because of its potency. And fortunately they haven't taken the more radical steps they were looking at in some of these areas.

Almost all of our Ecstacy is coming from Holland via Canada, and while we are trying to move as far in that direction as possible, and we need to work with them because I understand the difficulty at the border, not to mention localized issues, like I said, like cheese, the problems in the Vancouver Harbor reception and point of origin of what they are willing to do as what we might be able to do, Long Beach, Los Angeles or Seattle, with point of origin, are very difficult questions.

We are similar, and the goal in NAFTA is to push us more toward similarities and see the advantage of that cooperation, but there are some substantial difficulties. But organizations like yours pushing us in that direction hopefully will help do that.

Mr. SIMPSON. If I may, Mr. Chairman, I believe that the things that we need to do to create the zone of confidence between the United States and Canada can be accomplished without either nation sacrificing its political sovereignty. I think it is a really wonderful state of affairs that the United States and Canada have the luxury of disagreeing over soft wood lumber and cheese. That is, to me, a delightful situation.

I think the problems that lie between us and the sort of common security arrangement that we need to create are entirely manageable both politically and diplomatically and administratively, and there is no reason not to move forward quickly.

Mr. SOUDER. I wanted to also followup with Mr. Russell, because have you had experiences at both borders. Do you see—what kind of differences do you see that impact your firm differently on the north and south borders?

Mr. RUSSELL. We have seen a change over the past 17 years. In the past 2 years, the Mexican border has advanced in terms of infrastructure on the Mexican side rapidly. It is—there are differences in several core areas. Today a U.S. driver can cross into Canada, and a Canadian driver can cross into the United States.

But along the lines of the point you were just making, Mr. Chairman, there are differences. If a U.S. driver has been indicted on a nonpayment of alimony, as an example, in his county in Oklahoma, he is not allowed into Canada, whereas the U.S. laws and the—the immigration permission for Canadians crossing into the United States is different, and those differences basically have affected the way the borders have operated from a trucking standpoint in a relatively meaningful way.

The flow of freight between the two borders on the Canadian side after September 11th was quite difficult, for perhaps the next month or two, with the extensive delays, 20 hours, 15 hours, long lines of traffic. But due to the efforts of Customs and Immigration over the past several months, that has improved to almost the way it was before September 11th.

The Mexican border, again tremendous efforts by the Customs people, increasing the amount of intensity of reviews, and yet essentially very minor delays compared to prior to September 11th.

So the borders are different in many regards, but I think the philosophy that Mr. Simpson was talking about of creating a North American perimeter zone in certain areas makes a tremendous amount of sense.

Mr. SOUDER. Mr. Johnson, could you talk a little bit about the challenges we face on the southern border, because in the north I would assume that shipping is a little more seasonal; not completely, but a little more seasonal. The water sides of Mexico are complex. That is where a lot of our narcotics are coming in. The immigration question is a lot, because Mexico also can't control its south border. You referred to Panama and things moving through there.

Could you talk about your confidence in some of the security systems and how this would work——

Mr. JOHNSON. Sure.

Mr. SOUDER [continuing]. Both from the commerce standpoint and a potential terrorist?

Mr. JOHNSON. I think if we use the term "security system," we are being very generous in describing it as such, because it is not much of a system nor very secure. And I don't think there is a quick fix. I mean, it is human nature. We would like to get the quick fix. If we sit back and look at this objectively, the Al Qaeda members who tried to come into the United States came in two ways. They came in through the visa waiver program in Europe, and they went into Canada and then came in through Canada. We don't have any evidence of them coming across the Southern border.

I think, as I have talked to different people both in the counterterrorism community from State, from Customs, from FBI, and from some other agencies, I keep hearing the same thing, which is nobody has really sat down and agreed upon, within the U.S. Government, what secure border means, and so therefore we are pursuing a goal without even having it defined.

And I think there are legitimate concerns about how can you ensure that the commerce can move, because if—if anybody has sat and watched a container being loaded—I have been in Colon, Panama, and watched these things being stacked. I guess the only thing perhaps more exciting than that is sitting at an airport watching an X-ray machine. They are both very boring activities. It is repetition. And I think within this we can get to a point where we can put in place some screening systems. I mean, the cargo systems are being developed, but to get those developed technologically where they will process cargo containers at a very efficient rate is going to require an investment of resources that the private sector is not going to match. That is where government is going to have to step in and help move that along.

I don't think we are going to ever stop the illegal immigration of people coming across the border, because particularly in the Texas-New Mexico area and Arizona, it is too wide open. There are ways that people can get in there. But the threat that is posed from people trying to take advantage of the commercial transactions to me is one where we can use a combination of human behavior and incentives governing human behavior, making sure that people have an incentive to do a good job and equipping them with the technology to do it.

That said, getting that done, I think we are looking at a fairly 5 or 6-year effort at a minimum. That is assuming we commit the resources and we have a vision of what we are doing. What I am telling you now, based upon the facts here in government are telling me, there is no vision, and there is no consensus, and until you get those two issues addressed, I don't think you can deal with the others.

Mr. SOUDER. Thank you.

Mr. Cummings.

Mr. CUMMINGS. Yes. I just have just a few more questions.

Ms. Kelley, you talked about the briefings and joint operations like intelligence collection and analysis teams. You talked about how they had improved interagency cooperation. Do you think more of these briefings would cure some of the problems that proponents of consolidating agencies are attempting to achieve?

Ms. KELLEY. I think they would definitely help. I think they are not the only answer. The issue of a data base, a shared data base, that all law enforcement agencies have access to is one that I think needs to be followed through on, and it is one that I hear repeatedly is kind of the missing link for the front-line employees out in the field who are actually working the borders and the seaports and the airports, that is what they need is a single source of information for easy checking and access. That doesn't exist.

The briefings that I spoke about occur at the much higher levels here in Washington, DC, between the agencies. And I know that before September 11th, Customs, for example, was not included in those briefings, and they are today, and that has made a big difference in the communication that we see obviously on this important issue.

Mr. CUMMINGS. So you don't see reorganization as being necessary at all?

Ms. KELLEY. I don't. I think it always makes sense to look at how agencies are operating, if they are operating efficiently, but I think to reorganize or to consolidate and thinking that is the be-all and the end-all is the wrong answer. I think with everything that the agencies have that they are faced with today, having to focus their energy instead on a reorganization about who is in charge and about losing expertise—I continue to be very worried that each of the agencies have their very clear areas of expertise which I believe are undisputed, and to merge those and have them be diluted, I think, would be a disservice to the taxpayers and actually go against the goals that those who talk about consolidation are trying to achieve. It is not about consolidating, it is about providing the resources to the agencies to do the areas of expertise that they were formed and chartered to do many years ago.

Mr. CUMMINGS. These VACIS machines that are sitting and with nobody trained to use them, are there a lot of instances of that kind of thing where we have—first of all, is that pretty widespread, that particular machine?

Ms. KELLY . Yes. There are too many instances where the equipment is available—either is available and there is not enough staffing to run it, because you have to be trained to use it. Is a very intense process, so you need staffing. And so that is one issue is the staffing. And the second is equipment that is there, but needs maintenance. It needs to be repaired in some way. And the resources aren't there to do that, so it doesn't happen, it doesn't get used.

Mr. CUMMINGS. All right. We have got a vote. But I want to thank all of you for your testimony, and we will be following up with some written questions.

Mr. SOUDER. Thanks. I also want to thank you. I have a couple of additional questions I want to try to squeeze in here. Mr. Koch, first I want to thank not only you, but the others for giving us very specific things to chew on that we can try to get in the system here.

That in the point of origin, because that was an interesting concept, I assume that you also—there would be spot checks in transport, and you are saying the primary should be at port of origin. To what extent do you think that would be done by American agents, by—combination with private companies, and the companies—and representatives of the other nations at the point of origin?

Mr. KOCH. I would agree with Bonni Tischler's comment this morning. I think it is going to depend on the government and the port here that the U.S. Government is talking to. It could very easily be an analogy to the Canadian situation where we trust Canadian Customs, but would have some U.S. Customs people there to oversee the job, to look at the advanced data and say, hey, this one I want to look at; that one is fine, let it go.

I think we have to accept the fact that if we are going to put people in foreign ports, that they are going to expect reciprocity, and so we are going to have to be prepared to offer to foreign governments whatever we expect of them, because some foreign governments view American exports with some concern, too. Timothy McVeigh showed you can put something in a truck or a container and cause a lot of damage with it, and we cannot be insensitive to the fact that trade is bilateral, and what is going to be good for us has got to be good going in both directions.

There may be some countries where there is not effective cooperation, and then the government will have to figure out, how do you respond to that? But I think it is going to be a series of layers. It is going to be things like the TPAT program, where you find shippers who are willing to secure their supply chain from the time the container is stuffed through the transit to the port with the ocean carrier all of the way through. And for those people who don't participate in those kinds of programs, there has got to be consequences to greater risk of being inspected or delayed or whatever. It is going to be various layers that are going to be the answer to this. There won't be one single solution.

Mr. SOUDER. I think the record should show, too, what we have heard at a couple of the border crossings is that they actually have, in some cases, more narcotics going across our direction to Canada than vice versa, as well as money laundering. Often the BC Bud comes down, and the cocaine goes back. It isn't just a problem of coming at the United States, it is what we are putting out. And I think that was well said. Too often we don't acknowledge that. Everybody else is bad, and we are not. We have some problems in controlling things here, too.

I want to briefly—you each made, I believe, some comments on the mergers. And, I have one other question first. I believe, Mr. Johnson, you made a reference to the Coast Guard. What do you think is the single most important issue regarding maritime security that you believe our government isn't giving attention to so that as we look at new legislation——

Mr. JOHNSON. With the Coast Guard you do not have enough people to do the full inspection of the ships coming into the ports. That is simply stated. And the reason I favor looking at some sort of merger and putting these different agencies together is to harness the resources, to eliminate the redundancy, and to maximize the efficiency of all of the personnel.

Mr. SOUDER. You had a rather interesting alternative, because, that—that what is unbelievably confusing here is Coast Guard is under Transportation. Customs is under Treasury. We heard about the strawberries, which would be Ag, among others, seven agencies, that—and, of course, INS is Justice.

Part of the reason we have this committee with such broad oversight, probably the only oversight committee we have pieced it together. We have all drugs and narcotics because it got frustrating because it was in 22 different places. But we also have Commerce in with Justice, in with HHS and Education and HUD to try to look at different prongs of health and narcotics policy, but also because when we dealt with Justice issues and border issues, we can have Commerce underneath it. And this is just a microcosm of the mess—this is an oversight committee as well as some authorizing on narcotics. But you propose putting it all under Commerce where none of it currently is.

Mr. JOHNSON. I suggested putting it under Treasury, but the specifics, I think, can be battled over. But I think at the end of the day, look at it from a military standpoint. Within the military ultimately when you fight a war, there is a Commander in Chief. There are other agencies or units that support. And what you have right now with the U.S. Government in terms of protecting our borders is there is nobody in charge. There is no one person who is the CINC with support in command.

Mr. SOUDER. Would you agree that at a minimum that—your point in technology is something that just seems stupid, quite frankly, is that we are having multiple agencies develop different means to do the same thing; that at the very least the technology ought to be consolidated.

Mr. JOHNSON. Absolutely. I mean, immediately.

Mr. SOUDER. And data collection?

Mr. JOHNSON. Yes.

Mr. SOUDER. And if the other parts aren't consolidated, would you put those under Homeland Security, or would you put them under Justice?

Mr. JOHNSON. I think the Homeland Security Agency is a good concept, but Tom Ridge, unless he has money, he is ineffective. We watched with the drug czar for years, well-meaning people who get into that job, but they have no effective control over DOD, over Department of Justice, etc. So at the end of the day, the money—you know, the money in this town makes the world go around. If you get to write the checks, you get to direct the way the resources go.

So at the end of the day, I think there has to be somebody who is ultimately accountable to the Congress from a budget standpoint, because they can also enforce their will with the money.

Mr. SOUDER. The functional practicality at the borders, what we have seen is that INS and Customs agents are sharing duties; in fact, sometimes flipping who does what at different points of the day.

But the reason this is going to be so hard—and one of the things I want to make sure in this committee is that in—it has actually turned out as we look at terrorism, we are also following the narcotics question, but that the Coast Guard also has a search and safety component that historically has been the biggest. It has a fisheries component. The business community is going to be very reluctant to have the border become predominantly oriented toward security as opposed to trade. Those who are concerned about immigration as opposed to just terrorists are going to have huge concerns, and that is another block. Politically I don't really see how—not to mention just normal institutional committee jurisdiction problems these things often have. We have massive reports, but in practicality I just don't see, unless we are under multiple repeated attacks, that can happen that way.

And to the degree that we can get this scoped in and say, look, we have to do the technology, we have to do this—this security background check stuff where agencies—information floating around everywhere and not consolidated, or the types of terrible things that you mentioned, not to mention others that have been in the news media about we have the information, and it doesn't get into the system. That—we need to do those.

Do any of you have any additional comments you want to make before we close this down, and then we will also ask additional written questions. Any additional information that you or members of your association want to submit, because we are trying to build the case here, and we know the administration is debating on some of these things at this time. It is a good time to weigh in.

Mr. KOCH. Fully recognizing, Mr. Chairman, the difficulty of getting Congress to approve a legislative reorganization task, I still think there is plenty of issues that where there is organizational confusion in our government, where you don't need an act of Congress to get it fixed. The Office of Homeland Security was created to be a White House staff office. It could have the power of the White House to say, you have got this, you have got this, and you got this. And we are glad Governor Ridge is coming before you, because, I mean, presumably that office has the authority to make some of the—develop some of the answers to some of the questions you have heard today, which is what is the relationship between TSA and the Customs Service and the Coast Guard? Who owns container security? Who has got the job of negotiating with the foreign governments? Who owns the issue?

And while certainly legislation is one way to do it, it is not the only way to bring some clarity and resolution to the ambiguity that is holding things up.

Mr. SOUDER. I will say one of the things that I have learned in—when we dealt with narcotics overseas, that automatically takes you into trade and immigration. So we wound up consolidating things, because whenever we go over, we don't talk about all three things. We raise one; they raise another. We go back and forth. The other governments are also aligned and even often in more bureaucratic systems and overlap and trying to match up, so we have an international problem.

But I agree that—first off, we all agree we can do a whole lot better. The question is that hopefully under this administration we can see some of that.

Does anybody else have any additional comments?

Once again, thank you all for coming, and we will be in touch over the next few days.

[Whereupon, at 12:25 p.m., the subcommittee was adjourned.]

○

APEX
TP
9780160704048
76901945—93